ADVANTAGE

On My Own
PRACTICE WORKBOOK

Harcourt Brace & Company
Orlando • Atlanta • Austin • Boston • San Francisco • Chicago • Dallas • New York • Toronto • London
http://www.hbschool.com

W9-AUF-255

CONTENTS

One-to-One Correspondence

1.

2.

3.

4.

---

1. Draw one egg for each chicken.
2. Draw one carrot for each rabbit.

3. Draw one ball for each kitten.
4. Draw one banana for each monkey.

More and Fewer

1.

2.

3.

4.

1.–2. Draw flowers to show more flowers than butterflies.
3.–4. Draw leaves to show fewer leaves than bugs.

Numbers Through 5

1.
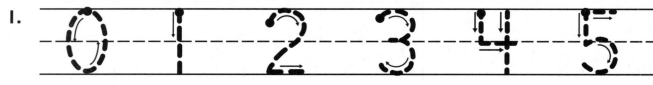

2.

3.

4.

5.

6.

7.

1. Write the numbers.
2.–7. Count. Write the number that tells how many.

Numbers Through 9

1.

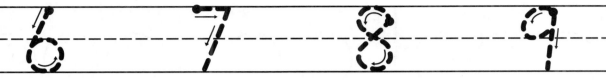

2.

3.

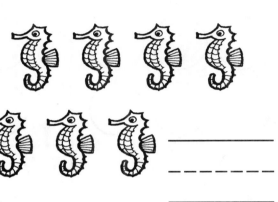

4.

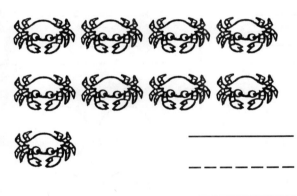

5.

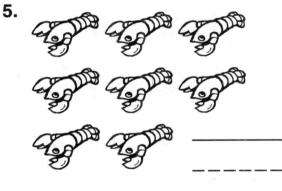

6.

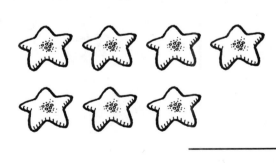

7.

1. Write the numbers.
2.–7. Count. Write the number that tells how many.

Ten

I.

2.

3.

4.

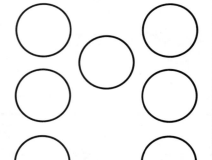

5.

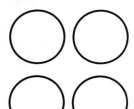

6.

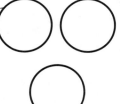

Write the number that tells how many.

Greater Than

1.

   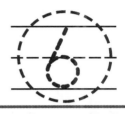

3

6

2.

_____

- - - - -

3.

_____

- - - - -

_____

- - - - -

4.

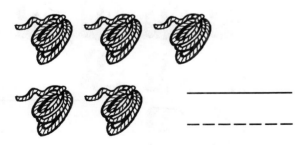

_____

- - - - -

_____

_____

- - - - -

_____

Count. Write the numbers.
Compare the groups. Circle the
number that is greater.

Less Than

1.

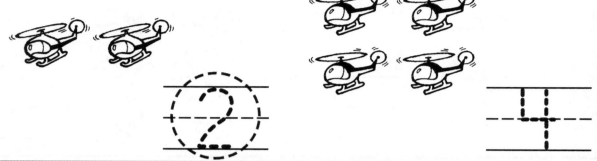

2.

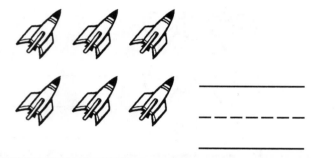

_ _ _ _ _ _ _   _ _ _ _ _ _ _

3.

_ _ _ _ _ _ _   _ _ _ _ _ _ _

4.

_ _ _ _ _ _ _   _ _ _ _ _ _ _

Count. Write the numbers. Compare the groups.
Circle the number that is less.

Order Through 10

1.

○○○○	○○○○○	◌◌◌◌◌◌
4	5	6

2.

	○○○○	○○○○○
	4	5

3.

○○	○○○	
2	3	

4.

○		○○○
1		3

5.

○○○○○	○○○○○○	
5	6	

6.

	○○○	○○○○
	3	4

Draw circles to show the missing number.
Write the number.

Ordinal Numbers

first   second   third   fourth   fifth

1.

2.

3.

4.

5.

1. Color the third animal yellow.
2. Color the fifth animal brown.
3. Color the second animal orange.

4. Color the fourth animal black.
5. Color the first animal red.

Modeling Addition Story Problems

Make up a story.
Use cubes to model the story.
Draw the cubes. Write how many there are in all.

1.

_____   _____   _____ in all

2.

_____   _____   _____ in all

▶ **Problem Solving**

Draw 🐦 and 🐤.
Show one way to make 6.
Write how many there are in all.

3.

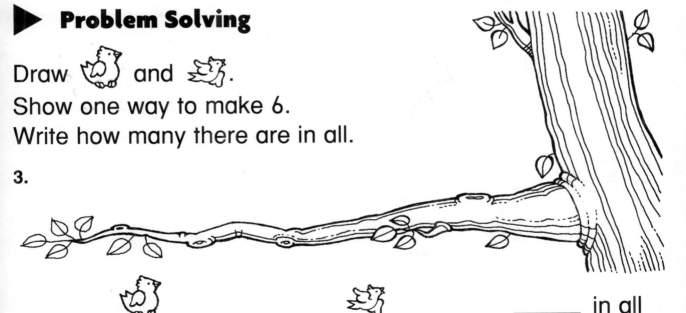

_____   _____   _____ in all

LESSON
1.2

Adding 1

▶ **Vocabulary**

Circle the **sum.**

1. 2 + 1 = 3

2. 0 + 1 = 1

Draw and color 1 more. Write the sum.

3.

3 + 1 = __4__
sum

4.

1 + 1 = __2__

5.

5 + 1 = __6__

6.

2 + 1 = __3__

7.

4 + 1 = __5__

8.

3 + 1 = __4__

Adding 2

Draw 2 more balloons.
Color them red.
Write the sum.

1.

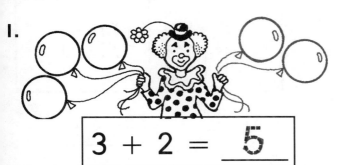

$3 + 2 = \underline{5}$

2.

$1 + 2 = \underline{3}$

3.

$2 + 2 = \underline{4}$

4.

$4 + 2 = \underline{6}$

5.

$3 + 2 = \underline{5}$

6.

$2 + 2 = \underline{4}$

▶ **Problem Solving**

Which group has 2 more than 3? Circle the group.

7.

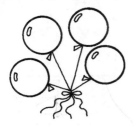

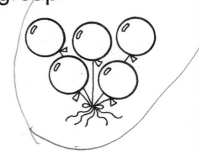

Using Pictures to Add

Write the sum.

1.

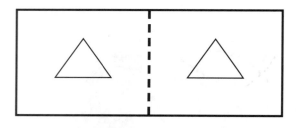

$1 + 1 =$ __2__

2.

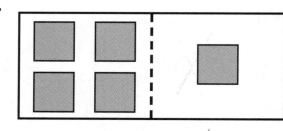

$4 + 1 =$ __5__

3.

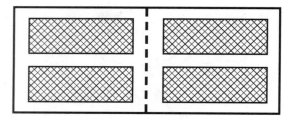

$2 + 2 =$ __4__

4.

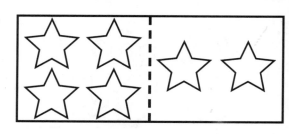

$4 + 2 =$ __6__

5.

$3 + 2 =$ __5__

6.

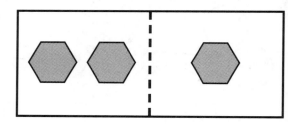

$2 + 1 =$ __3__

7.

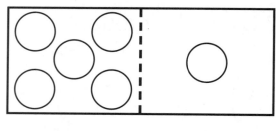

$5 + 1 =$ __6__

8.

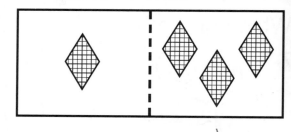

$1 + 3 =$ __4__

Writing Addition Sentences

Write the addition sentence.

1.

__4__ + __2__ = __6__

2.

__2__ + __1__ = __2__

3.

__3__ + __2__ = __5__

4.

__1__ + __3__ = __4__

5.

__2__ + __2__ = __4__

6.

__1__ + __1__ = __2__

▶ **Problem Solving**

Draw. Write the addition sentence.

7. Draw 1 yellow .
Draw 2 blue 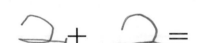.

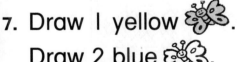

__1__ + __2__ = __3__

8. Draw 3 orange .
Draw 1 green 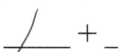.

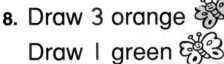

__3__ + __1__ = __4__

Modeling Subtraction Story Problems

Tell a story to a friend.
Use counters to model the story.
Draw the counters. Write how many are left.

1.

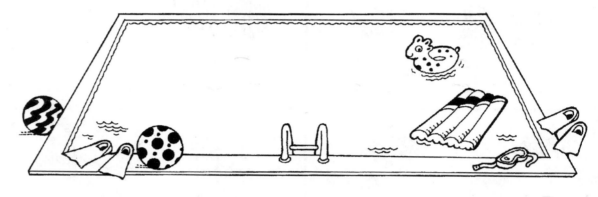

_____ swimmers   _____ go away   _____ are left

2.

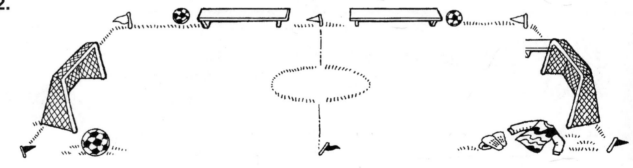

_____ soccer players   _____ go away   _____ are left

3.

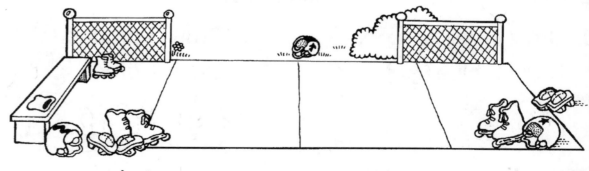

_____ skaters   _____ go away   _____ are left

Name Zane 8/21/08

LESSON 2.2

Subtracting 1

Vocabulary

Circle the **subtraction sentence**.

1. 2 + 1 = 3 2 − 1 = 1

Cross out 1 picture. Write how many are left.

2. 3 − 1 = 2

3. 4 − 1 = 3

4. 2 − 1 = 1

5. 5 − 1 = 4

Problem Solving

Tell a story. Write how many are left.

6.

5 − 1 = 4

7.

4 − 1 = 3

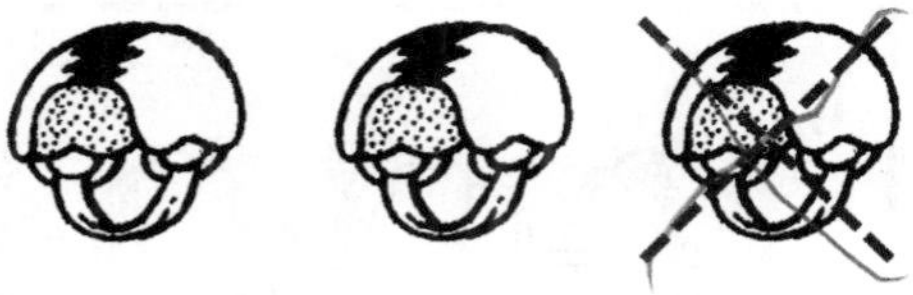

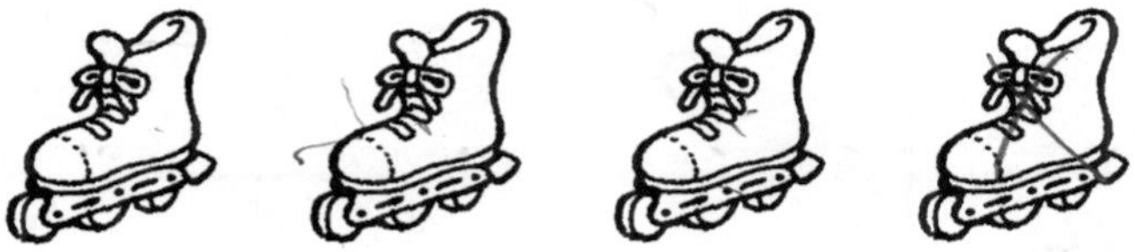

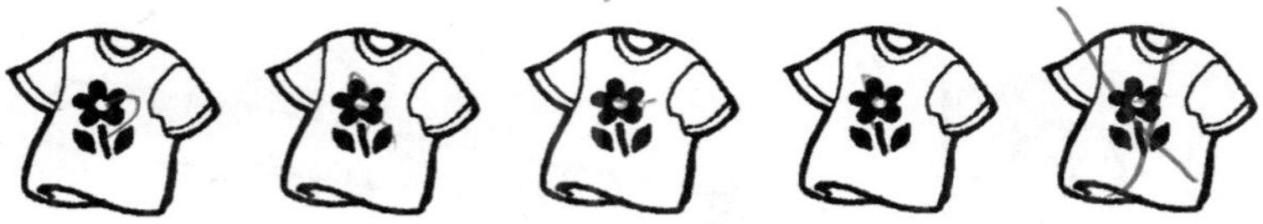

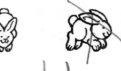

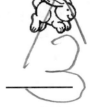

Subtracting 2

Cross out pictures to show the
subtraction sentence. Write how many are left.

1.

$5 - 2 = \underline{3}$

2.

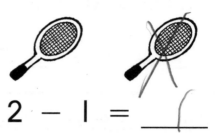

$2 - 1 = \underline{1}$

3.

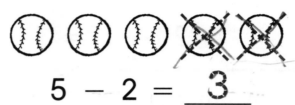

$1 - 1 = \underline{}$

4.

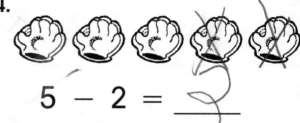

$5 - 2 = \underline{3}$

5.

$4 - 2 = \underline{2}$

6.

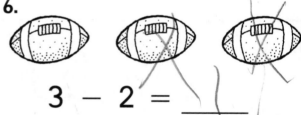

$3 - 2 = \underline{1}$

7.

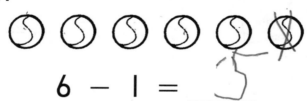

$6 - 1 = \underline{5}$

8.

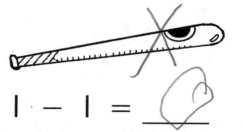

$1 - 1 = \underline{}$

9.

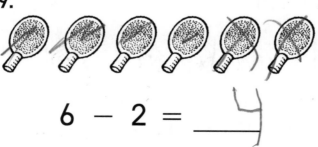

$6 - 2 = \underline{4}$

10.

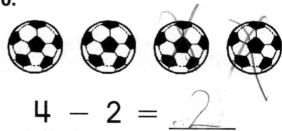

$4 - 2 = \underline{2}$

Writing Subtraction Sentences

▶ **Vocabulary**

Circle the **difference**.

1.
$$4 - 2 = \boxed{2}$$

2.
$$6 - 2 = \boxed{4}$$

Write a subtraction sentence to show the difference.

3.

$$\underline{4} - \underline{2} = \underline{2}$$
difference

4.

$$\underline{3} - \underline{1} = \underline{2}$$

5.

$$\underline{6} - \underline{3} = \underline{3}$$

6.

$$\underline{5} - \underline{2} = \underline{3}$$

7.

$$\underline{2} - \underline{1} = \underline{1}$$

8.
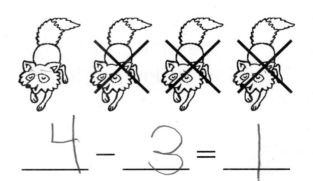

$$\underline{4} - \underline{3} = \underline{1}$$

Problem Solving • Make a Model

Add or subtract. Use counters.
Draw the counters.

1. 4 ducks are swimming.
   I more comes.
   How many in all?

    __5__ ducks

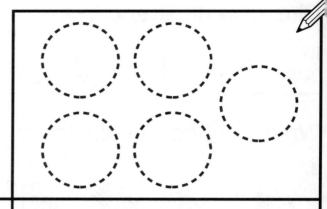

2. 6 kittens are playing.
   4 run away.
   How many are left?

    __2__ kittens

3. 3 bees are on a flower.
   2 more come.
   How many in all?

    __5__ bees

4. 3 turtles are on a log.
   I goes into the water.
   How many are left?

    __2__ turtles

Order Property

Use two-color counters and Workmat 2 to find each sum. Circle the two problems that have the same sum.

1.
$2 + 1 = 3$ $1 + 0 = 1$ $1 + 2 = 3$

2.
$0 + 3 = 3$ $3 + 1 = 4$ $1 + 3 = 4$

3.
$2 + 4 = 6$ $4 + 1 = 5$ $4 + 2 = 6$

4.
$3 + 1 = 4$ $3 + 0 = 3$ $0 + 3 = 3$

5.
$3 + 2 = 5$ $2 + 3 = 5$ $2 + 0 = 2$

6.
$5 + 1 = 6$ $1 + 5 = 6$ $3 + 4 = 7$

▶ **Problem Solving**

Circle the cubes that show the same number.

7.
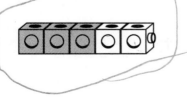
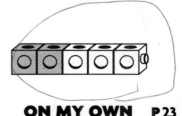

Addition Combinations

Use two-color counters and Workmat 2.
Find ways to make the sums.

1. __2__ + __5__ = 7

2. __3__ + __4__ = 7

3. _____ + _____ = 7

4. _____ + _____ = 7

5. _____ + _____ = 7

6. _____ + _____ = 7

7. _____ + _____ = 8

8. _____ + _____ = 8

9. _____ + _____ = 8

10. _____ + _____ = 8

11. _____ + _____ = 8

12. _____ + _____ = 8

▶ **Problem Solving**

Draw fish in each bowl to make the sum.
Write the numbers.

13.
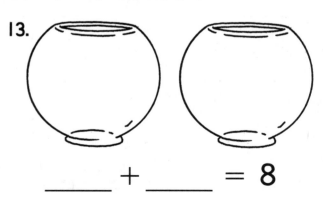

_____ + _____ = 8

14.
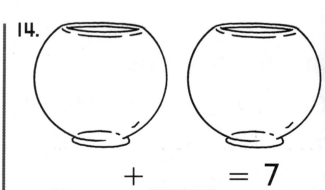

_____ + _____ = 7

More Addition Combinations

Use two colors of cubes to find
ways to make the sums.
Color to show the ways.

1.

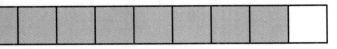

$\underline{8} + \underline{1} = 9$

2.

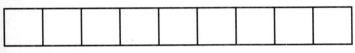

$\underline{} + \underline{} = 9$

3.

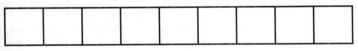

$\underline{} + \underline{} = 9$

4.

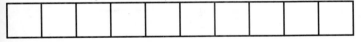

$\underline{} + \underline{} = 9$

5.

$\underline{9} + \underline{1} = 10$

6.

$\underline{} + \underline{} = 10$

7.

$\underline{} + \underline{} = 10$

8.

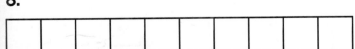

$\underline{} + \underline{} = 10$

Horizontal and Vertical Addition

Complete.

1.

$\underline{2} + \underline{1} = \underline{3}$

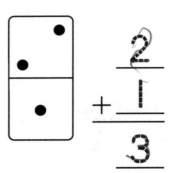

$\begin{array}{r} 2 \\ + 1 \\ \hline 3 \end{array}$

2.

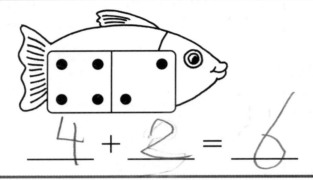

$\underline{4} + \underline{2} = \underline{6}$

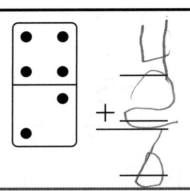

$\begin{array}{r} 4 \\ + 2 \\ \hline 6 \end{array}$

3.

$\underline{3} + \underline{4} = \underline{7}$

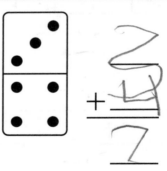

$\begin{array}{r} 3 \\ + 4 \\ \hline 7 \end{array}$

▶ **Problem Solving**

Write the sum.

4. Circle the sum that is greater.

$8 + 2 = 10$

$8 + 1 = 9$

5. Circle the sum that is less.

$7 + 1 = 8$

$7 + 0 = 7$

Problem Solving • Make a Model

▶ **Vocabulary**

Circle the **cent** sign.

1.   + $ –   ⊙ ¢

Mark an **X** on the **penny**.

2.

Use pennies to show each price.
Draw them. Write the total amount.

3. 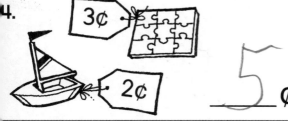   ___7___ ¢

4.    ___5___ ¢

5.    ___9___ ¢

6. 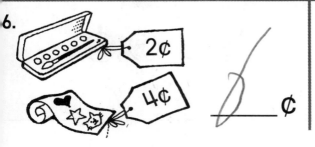   ___6___ ¢

Counting On 1 and 2

▶ **Vocabulary**

Count on to add.

1.
$\begin{array}{r} 4 \\ +\ 1 \\ \hline 5 \end{array}$ Count on 1. **5** $\begin{array}{r} 7 \\ +\ 2 \\ \hline 9 \end{array}$ Count on 2. **8,9** $\begin{array}{r} 6 \\ +\ 1 \\ \hline 7 \end{array}$ Count on 1. **7**

2.
$\begin{array}{r} 4 \\ +\ 2 \\ \hline 6 \end{array}$ $\begin{array}{r} 5 \\ +\ 1 \\ \hline 6 \end{array}$ $\begin{array}{r} 8 \\ +\ 2 \\ \hline 10 \end{array}$ $\begin{array}{r} 6 \\ +\ 1 \\ \hline 7 \end{array}$ $\begin{array}{r} 2 \\ +\ 1 \\ \hline 3 \end{array}$

3.
$\begin{array}{r} 2 \\ +\ 2 \\ \hline 4 \end{array}$ $\begin{array}{r} 1 \\ +\ 2 \\ \hline 3 \end{array}$ $\begin{array}{r} 8 \\ +\ 1 \\ \hline 9 \end{array}$ $\begin{array}{r} 1 \\ +\ 1 \\ \hline 2 \end{array}$ $\begin{array}{r} 7 \\ +\ 2 \\ \hline 9 \end{array}$

4.
$\begin{array}{r} 5 \\ +\ 1 \\ \hline 6 \end{array}$ $\begin{array}{r} 7 \\ +\ 2 \\ \hline 9 \end{array}$ $\begin{array}{r} 4 \\ +\ 1 \\ \hline 5 \end{array}$ $\begin{array}{r} 2 \\ +\ 2 \\ \hline 4 \end{array}$ $\begin{array}{r} 6 \\ +\ 1 \\ \hline 7 \end{array}$

▶ **Problem Solving**

Tell a story. Write the addition sentence.

5.

$3 \oplus 1 \ominus 4$

6.

$7 \oplus 2 \ominus 9$

Counting On 3

Count on to add.

1.

$$\begin{array}{r} 6 \\ +3 \\ \hline 9 \end{array}$$

$$\begin{array}{r} 5 \\ +1 \\ \hline \end{array}$$

$$\begin{array}{r} 3 \\ +2 \\ \hline \end{array}$$

$$\begin{array}{r} 1 \\ +3 \\ \hline \end{array}$$

$$\begin{array}{r} 5 \\ +2 \\ \hline \end{array}$$

2.

$$\begin{array}{r} 7 \\ +3 \\ \hline \end{array}$$

$$\begin{array}{r} 6 \\ +2 \\ \hline \end{array}$$

$$\begin{array}{r} 3 \\ +3 \\ \hline \end{array}$$

$$\begin{array}{r} 6 \\ +1 \\ \hline \end{array}$$

$$\begin{array}{r} 1 \\ +2 \\ \hline \end{array}$$

3.

$$\begin{array}{r} 4 \\ +3 \\ \hline \end{array}$$

$$\begin{array}{r} 4 \\ +2 \\ \hline \end{array}$$

$$\begin{array}{r} 2 \\ +2 \\ \hline \end{array}$$

$$\begin{array}{r} 2 \\ +3 \\ \hline \end{array}$$

$$\begin{array}{r} 7 \\ +1 \\ \hline \end{array}$$

4.

$$\begin{array}{r} 6 \\ +3 \\ \hline \end{array}$$

$$\begin{array}{r} 5 \\ +3 \\ \hline \end{array}$$

$$\begin{array}{r} 2 \\ +1 \\ \hline \end{array}$$

$$\begin{array}{r} 8 \\ +1 \\ \hline \end{array}$$

$$\begin{array}{r} 7 \\ +2 \\ \hline \end{array}$$

▶ **Problem Solving**

Solve.

5. Sara has 5 pencils. Tom has 3 pencils. How many pencils do Sara and Tom have in all?

___8___ pencils

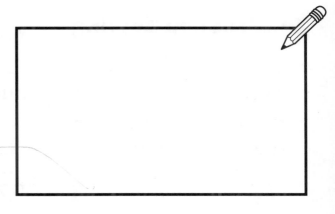

Doubles

▶ **Vocabulary**

Circle the **doubles**.

1.   (3 + 2 = 5)   3 + 3 = 6
_____

Make each picture show a double.
Write the doubles fact.

2.

_5_ + _5_ = _10_

3.
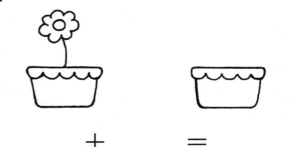

___ + ___ = ___

4.

___ + ___ = ___

5.
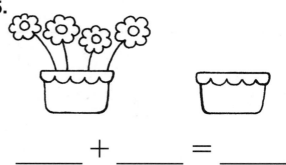

___ + ___ = ___

▶ **Problem Solving**

6. Jesse has 3 apples.
Matt has double this amount.
How many apples
does Matt have?

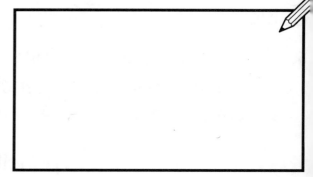

____ apples

Addition Facts Practice

Write the sum. Circle the doubles.

1.

$3 + 4 = \underline{7}$　　$5 + 1 = \underline{6}$　　$\left(4 + 4 = \underline{8}\right)$

2.

$2 + 4 = \underline{}$　　$3 + 3 = \underline{}$　　$4 + 1 = \underline{}$

3.

$0 + 2 = \underline{}$　　$6 + 2 = \underline{}$　　$1 + 1 = \underline{}$

4.

$2 + 2 = \underline{}$　　$3 + 2 = \underline{}$　　$7 + 1 = \underline{}$

5.

$$\begin{array}{r} 3 \\ +1 \\ \hline \end{array} \qquad \begin{array}{r} 1 \\ +1 \\ \hline \end{array} \qquad \begin{array}{r} 5 \\ +5 \\ \hline \end{array} \qquad \begin{array}{r} 6 \\ +2 \\ \hline \end{array} \qquad \begin{array}{r} 6 \\ +3 \\ \hline \end{array}$$

6.

$$\begin{array}{r} 3 \\ +3 \\ \hline \end{array} \qquad \begin{array}{r} 4 \\ +1 \\ \hline \end{array} \qquad \begin{array}{r} 2 \\ +5 \\ \hline \end{array} \qquad \begin{array}{r} 4 \\ +4 \\ \hline \end{array} \qquad \begin{array}{r} 2 \\ +1 \\ \hline \end{array}$$

▶ **Problem Solving**

7. Doug has 3 cars.
Jim has 3 cars.
How many cars do Doug
and Jim have in all?

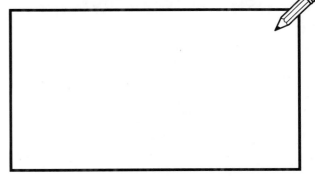

_____ cars

Problem Solving • Draw a Picture

Draw pictures to solve.

1. 4 kittens are white.
2 kittens are black.
How many kittens in all?

_6_

2. David has 6 yo-yos.
He gives away 2.
How many are left?

_____

3. Jeremy has 3 red balloons.
Ross has 3 blue balloons.
How many balloons in all?

_____

4. Heather has 7 flowers.
She gives away 2.
How many are left?

_____

Subtraction Combinations

Use counters. Write ways to subtract.

1. $7 - \underline{\ 7\ } = \underline{\ 0\ }$ 2. $8 - \underline{\quad} = \underline{\quad}$

3. $7 - \underline{\quad} = \underline{\quad}$ 4. $8 - \underline{\quad} = \underline{\quad}$

5. $7 - \underline{\quad} = \underline{\quad}$ 6. $8 - \underline{\quad} = \underline{\quad}$

Subtract.

7.
$$\begin{array}{r} 7 \\ -\ 4 \\ \hline 3 \end{array} \qquad \begin{array}{r} 6 \\ -\ 2 \\ \hline \end{array} \qquad \begin{array}{r} 7 \\ -\ 7 \\ \hline \end{array} \qquad \begin{array}{r} 8 \\ -\ 4 \\ \hline \end{array} \qquad \begin{array}{r} 7 \\ -\ 6 \\ \hline \end{array} \qquad \begin{array}{r} 8 \\ -\ 3 \\ \hline \end{array}$$

8.
$$\begin{array}{r} 5 \\ -\ 3 \\ \hline \end{array} \qquad \begin{array}{r} 8 \\ -\ 7 \\ \hline \end{array} \qquad \begin{array}{r} 7 \\ -\ 5 \\ \hline \end{array} \qquad \begin{array}{r} 3 \\ -\ 1 \\ \hline \end{array} \qquad \begin{array}{r} 7 \\ -\ 0 \\ \hline \end{array} \qquad \begin{array}{r} 7 \\ -\ 1 \\ \hline \end{array}$$

9.
$$\begin{array}{r} 6 \\ -\ 3 \\ \hline \end{array} \qquad \begin{array}{r} 8 \\ -\ 0 \\ \hline \end{array} \qquad \begin{array}{r} 7 \\ -\ 2 \\ \hline \end{array} \qquad \begin{array}{r} 8 \\ -\ 8 \\ \hline \end{array} \qquad \begin{array}{r} 9 \\ -\ 7 \\ \hline \end{array} \qquad \begin{array}{r} 8 \\ -\ 5 \\ \hline \end{array}$$

 Problem Solving

Which answer will be less than 5?
Circle the problem. Solve to check.

10. $8 - 4 = \underline{\quad}$ $8 - 2 = \underline{\quad}$ $8 - 1 = \underline{\quad}$

More Subtraction Combinations

Use counters. Write ways to subtract.

1. $9 - \underline{0} = \underline{9}$

2. $10 - \underline{} = \underline{}$

3. $9 - \underline{} = \underline{}$

4. $10 - \underline{} = \underline{}$

5. $9 - \underline{} = \underline{}$

6. $10 - \underline{} = \underline{}$

7. $9 - \underline{} = \underline{}$

8. $10 - \underline{} = \underline{}$

9. $9 - \underline{} = \underline{}$

10. $10 - \underline{} = \underline{}$

11. $9 - \underline{} = \underline{}$

12. $10 - \underline{} = \underline{}$

13. $9 - \underline{} = \underline{}$

14. $10 - \underline{} = \underline{}$

15. $9 - \underline{} = \underline{}$

16. $10 - \underline{} = \underline{}$

Vertical Subtraction

Complete.

1.

$$4 - 1 = 3$$

$$\begin{array}{r} 4 \\ -\ 1 \\ \hline 3 \end{array}$$

2.

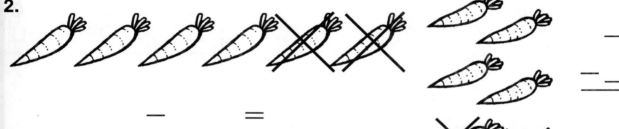

_____ — _____ = _____

_____
—
_____
_____

3.

_____ — _____ = _____

_____
—
_____

▶ **Problem Solving**

Add or subtract. Circle the answer that is greater.

4. Sam has 7 balloons. _____
He breaks 2.
How many
are left?

_____

Liz has 3 fish. _____
She buys 1 more.
How many
does she have?

_____

Fact Families

▶ **Vocabulary**

Circle the sentence that does not belong in the **fact family**.

1.
$$6+3=9 \qquad 9-5=4$$
$$3+6=9 \qquad 9-6=3$$
$$9-3=6$$

Add or subtract. Write the numbers in the fact family.

2.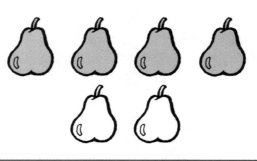

$$\begin{array}{r} 4 \\ +2 \\ \hline 6 \end{array} \qquad \begin{array}{r} 2 \\ +4 \\ \hline 6 \end{array} \qquad \begin{array}{r} 6 \\ -2 \\ \hline 4 \end{array} \qquad \begin{array}{r} 6 \\ -4 \\ \hline 2 \end{array}$$

| 4 | 2 | 6 |

3.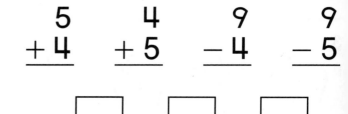

$$\begin{array}{r} 5 \\ +4 \\ \hline \end{array} \qquad \begin{array}{r} 4 \\ +5 \\ \hline \end{array} \qquad \begin{array}{r} 9 \\ -4 \\ \hline \end{array} \qquad \begin{array}{r} 9 \\ -5 \\ \hline \end{array}$$

☐   ☐   ☐

4.

$$\begin{array}{r} 5 \\ +3 \\ \hline \end{array} \qquad \begin{array}{r} 3 \\ +5 \\ \hline \end{array} \qquad \begin{array}{r} 8 \\ -3 \\ \hline \end{array} \qquad \begin{array}{r} 8 \\ -5 \\ \hline \end{array}$$

☐   ☐   ☐

▶ **Problem Solving**

5. Tell a story. Write the numbers in the fact family.

 ☐   ☐   ☐

Subtracting to Compare

Draw lines to match. Subtract to compare.
Write how many more.

1.

$7 - 5 =$ __2__

__2__ more

2.

$6 - 2 =$ _____

_____ more

3.

$5 - 4 =$ _____

_____ more

4.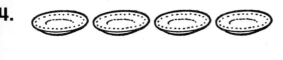

$4 - 1 =$ _____

_____ more

▶ **Problem Solving**

Solve.

5. You have 8 🌸. _____

You have 6 🌷. − _____

How many more
🌸 do you have? _____

6. You have 6 🔒. _____

You have 1 🔑. − _____

How many more
🔑 do you need? _____

Counting Back 1 and 2

▶ Vocabulary

Use the number line.
Count back to subtract.

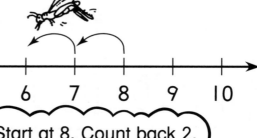

1.

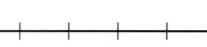

0 1 2 3 4 5 6 7 8 9 10

$8 - 2 = \underline{6}$

Start at 8. Count back 2.
Where are you?

2.

0 1 2 3 4 5

$5 - 1 = \underline{}$

3.

0 1 2 3 4 5

$3 - 2 = \underline{}$

4.

0 1 2 3 4 5

$4 - 2 = \underline{}$

5.

0 1 2 3 4 5

$4 - 1 = \underline{}$

6.

5 6 7 8 9 10

$10 - 2 = \underline{}$

7.

5 6 7 8 9 10

$9 - 2 = \underline{}$

▶ Problem Solving

Solve.

8. Sophie had 5 balloons.
3 blew away.
How many balloons does
she have left?

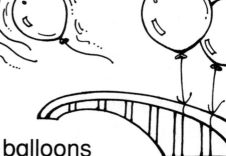

_____ balloons

Counting Back 3

Use the number line. Count back to subtract.

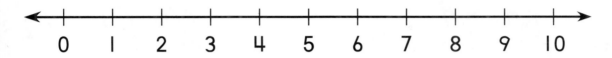

$$0 \quad 1 \quad 2 \quad 3 \quad 4 \quad 5 \quad 6 \quad 7 \quad 8 \quad 9 \quad 10$$

1.

$8 - 3 = \underline{5}$ $9 - 3 = \underline{}$ $6 - 3 = \underline{}$

2.

$4 - 2 = \underline{}$ $7 - 1 = \underline{}$ $9 - 2 = \underline{}$

3.

$3 - 1 = \underline{}$ $3 - 3 = \underline{}$ $2 - 1 = \underline{}$

4.

$$\begin{array}{cccccc} 7 & 8 & 4 & 8 & 7 & 4 \\ -3 & -1 & -2 & -3 & -1 & -3 \\ \hline \end{array}$$

5.

$$\begin{array}{cccccc} 5 & 2 & 3 & 6 & 4 & 6 \\ -2 & -1 & -3 & -2 & -3 & -1 \\ \hline \end{array}$$

▶ **Problem Solving**

Solve.

6. Use these numbers.
Write a subtraction sentence.

10   7   3

____ − ____ = ____

Subtracting Zero

Subtract. Circle all the zero facts.

1.

$$\begin{array}{r} 6 \\ -\ 6 \\ \hline 0 \end{array}$$

$$\begin{array}{r} 6 \\ -\ 0 \\ \hline 6 \end{array}$$

2.

$$\begin{array}{r} 9 \\ -9 \\ \hline \end{array} \qquad \begin{array}{r} 5 \\ -0 \\ \hline \end{array} \qquad \begin{array}{r} 8 \\ -3 \\ \hline \end{array} \qquad \begin{array}{r} 5 \\ -5 \\ \hline \end{array} \qquad \begin{array}{r} 3 \\ -3 \\ \hline \end{array} \qquad \begin{array}{r} 7 \\ -3 \\ \hline \end{array}$$

3.

$$\begin{array}{r} 7 \\ -2 \\ \hline \end{array} \qquad \begin{array}{r} 8 \\ -8 \\ \hline \end{array} \qquad \begin{array}{r} 5 \\ -4 \\ \hline \end{array} \qquad \begin{array}{r} 4 \\ -4 \\ \hline \end{array} \qquad \begin{array}{r} 5 \\ -1 \\ \hline \end{array} \qquad \begin{array}{r} 3 \\ -0 \\ \hline \end{array}$$

4.

$$\begin{array}{r} 4 \\ -1 \\ \hline \end{array} \qquad \begin{array}{r} 7 \\ -7 \\ \hline \end{array} \qquad \begin{array}{r} 3 \\ -2 \\ \hline \end{array} \qquad \begin{array}{r} 10 \\ -1 \\ \hline \end{array} \qquad \begin{array}{r} 2 \\ -1 \\ \hline \end{array} \qquad \begin{array}{r} 9 \\ -9 \\ \hline \end{array}$$

▶ **Problem Solving**

Write the subtraction sentence.

5.

_____ − _____ = _____

Facts Practice

Add or subtract. Fill in the numbers.

1.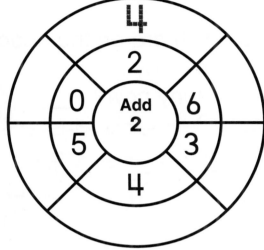

2.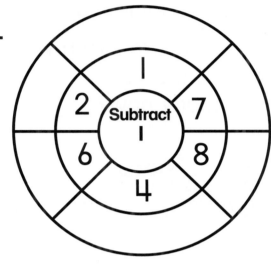

3.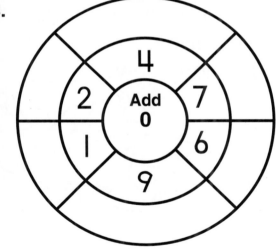

4.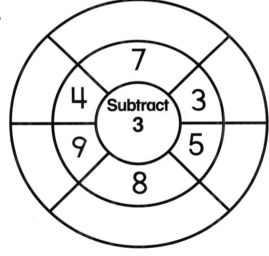

▶ **Problem Solving**

Circle **add** or **subtract**. Solve.

5. Carol has 6 flowers.
   She picks 4 more.
   How many flowers does she have in all? _____ flowers

   add   **subtract**

Problem Solving • Draw a Picture

Add or subtract.
Draw more things, or cross things out.

1. 3 buckets are in a row.
Make 2 more.
How many now? __5__

2. 6 starfish are on the beach.
2 swim away.
How many now? _____

3. I chair is in the sand.
Make I more.
How many now? _____

4. 4 seagulls are walking.
I flies away.
How many now? _____

5. 5 puppies are sleeping.
3 run away.
How many now? _____

6. 2 balls are in the yard.
Make 2 more.
How many now? _____

Solid Figures

▶ **Vocabulary**

Draw a line to match each word with a figure.

1.

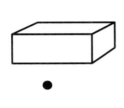

•   •   •

•   •   •

sphere   **rectangular prism**   **cone**

Color the figures that have the same shape.

2.

   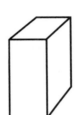

3.

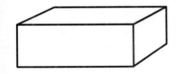      

4.

▶ **Problem Solving**

5. I am a solid figure.
   I can roll. Circle me.

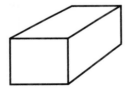

More Solid Figures

▶ **Vocabulary**

Draw a line to match each word with a figure.

1.

cylinder •   •

cube •   •

pyramid •   •

Color the objects that have the same shape.

2.

3.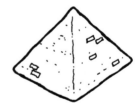

4.

▶ **Problem Solving**

Color the figures that are cylinders.
Mark an **X** on the figures that are not cylinders.

5.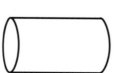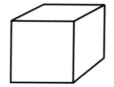

Sorting Solid Figures

 **stack**  **slide**  **roll**

Color each figure that will stack.

1.

Color each figure that will slide.

2.

Color each figure that will roll.

3.

Color each figure that will roll and stack.

4.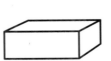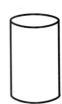

▶ Problem Solving

Color the figure that will stack, slide, and roll.

5.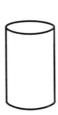

More Sorting Solid Figures

Circle each figure that goes with the sentence.

1. No face is flat.

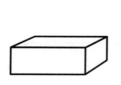

2. All faces are flat.

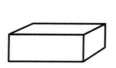

3. Only 1 face is flat.

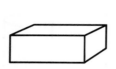

4. Only 2 faces are flat.

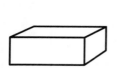   

▶ **Problem Solving**

5. Find all the △.
   Write how many.

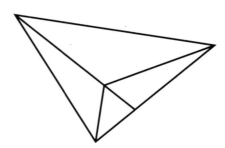

_____

Name _____

Problem Solving • Make a Model

Build the model. Write how many cubes you used.

1.

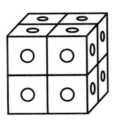

_____8_____ cubes

2.

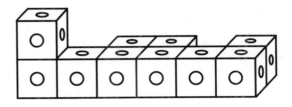

_____ cubes

3.

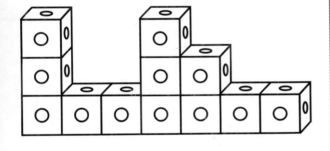

_____ cubes

4.

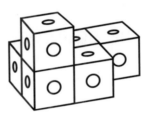

_____ cubes

5.

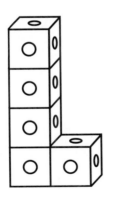

_____ cubes

6.

_____ cubes

Plane Figures

▶ **Vocabulary**

Color each **flat face**.

1.

  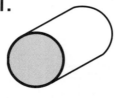 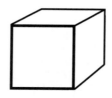 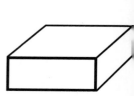

circle   **square**   **triangle**   **rectangle**

---

2. Color the triangles.

    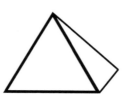

---

3. Color the squares.

  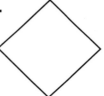

---

4. Color the circles.

      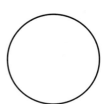

▶ **Problem Solving**

5. Color the figure that has all **flat faces**.

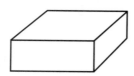   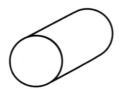

Sorting Plane Figures

Trace each side. blue ▷
Draw a ◯ on each corner. red ▷
Write how many sides and corners.

1.

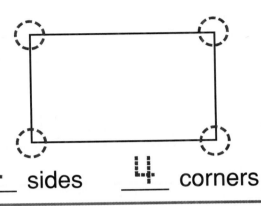

__4__ sides   __4__ corners

2.

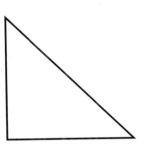

____ sides   ____ corners

3.

____ sides   ____ corners

4.

____ sides   ____ corners

▶ **Problem Solving**

5. Circle the figure that has 4 corners and 4 sides.

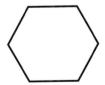

6. Circle the figure that has 5 corners and 5 sides.

 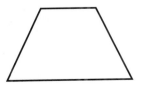

Congruence

Color the figures that are the same size and shape.

1.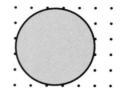

2.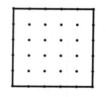

3.

4.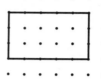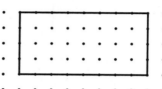

▶ **Problem Solving**

Circle the figure.

5. I have no corners.
I have no sides.
What am I?

6. I have 4 corners.
I have 4 sides.
What am I?

Symmetry

Draw a line to make two sides that match.

1.
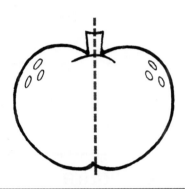

2.
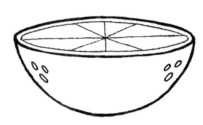

3.
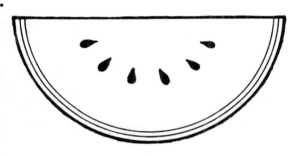

4.

5.

6.

▶ Problem Solving

7. Circle the figure with two parts that do not match.

Open and Closed

▶ Vocabulary

1. Circle the **open** figure.

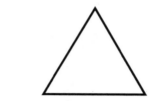

2. Circle the **closed** figure.

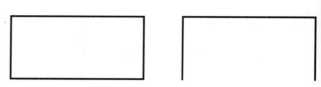

Color each closed figure. Circle each open figure.

3.

 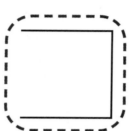  

4.

 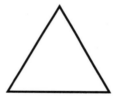 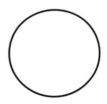 

5.

   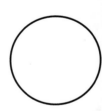

▶ Problem Solving

Circle the letters that are open figures.

6.

E   B   R   S   D   C

Inside, Outside, On

▶ **Vocabulary**

green **inside**   blue **outside**   red **on**

Color the squares.

1.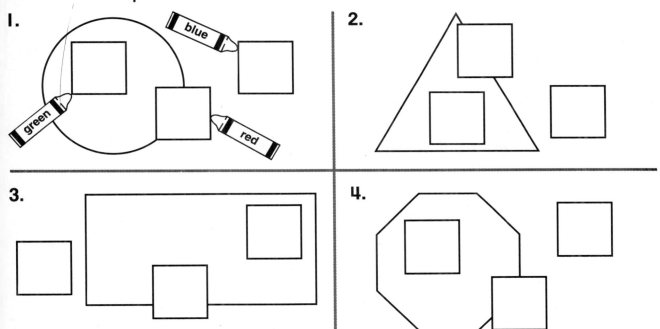

2.

3.

4.

▶ **Problem Solving**

5. Which shape is inside both circles? Color the shape.

Problem Solving • Draw a Picture

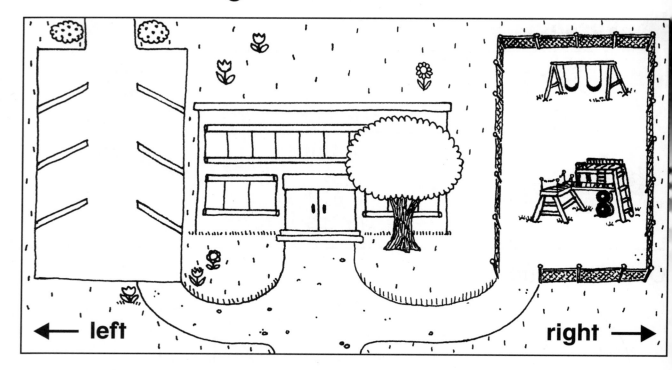

left →   right ←

Draw to complete the map.

1. Draw a 🚗 to the left of the 🏢.

2. Draw a 📪 to the right of the 🌳.

3. Draw two 🧑 in the ▦.

Circle **left** or **right**.

4. You walk to the 🚗 from the 🏢.

   Which way are you going?

   left   right

5. You go from the 🌳 to the 📪.

   Which way are you going?

   left   right

Positions on a Grid

Start at ☆. Follow directions to draw shapes on the grid.

1.

Right	Up	Draw
5	6	○
2	7	□

Right	Up	Draw
4	3	△
1	4	▭

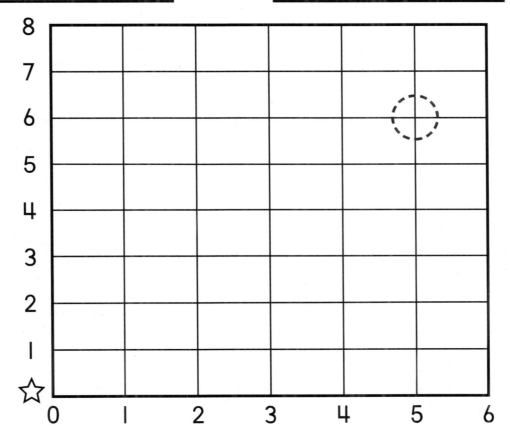

Up ↑

Right →

☆

▶ Problem Solving

Look at the grid. Circle the correct shape.

2. What shape is to the
left of the triangle?

3. Which shape is farther
to the right?

Identifying Patterns

Color the R stars red.
Color the B stars blue.
Color the Y stars yellow.
Read the pattern. Then color to continue it.

I.

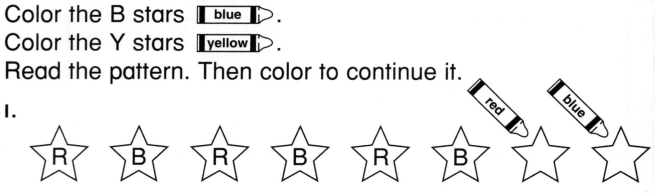

2.

3.

4.

▶ Problem Solving

5. Tina drew these shapes.

Alan drew these shapes.

Circle the shapes that show a pattern.

Reproducing and Extending Patterns

Color the squares to copy and continue the pattern.

1.

red	blue	red	blue	red	blue		

red	blue	red	blue	red	blue		

2.

blue	red	blue	red	blue	red

3.

red	red	blue	red	red	blue

▶ **Problem Solving**

4. Make your own pattern. Use red and blue crayons.

5. Write a number to continue the pattern.

3	4	5	3	4	5	___

Making and Extending Patterns

Use shapes to continue the pattern.
Then use the same shapes to make a different pattern.
Draw the shapes to show your new pattern.

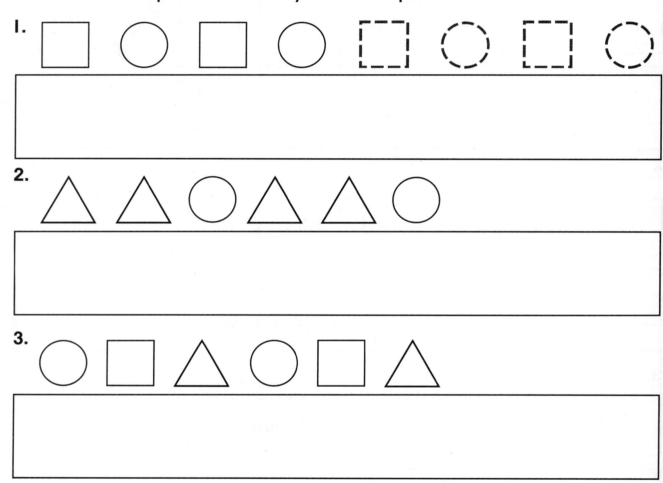

1.

2.

3.

▶ Problem Solving

Draw the missing shapes to complete the pattern.

4.

5.

Analyzing Patterns

Find the mistake in the pattern. Cross it out.
Then use shapes to show the pattern the correct way.
Draw and color the shapes.

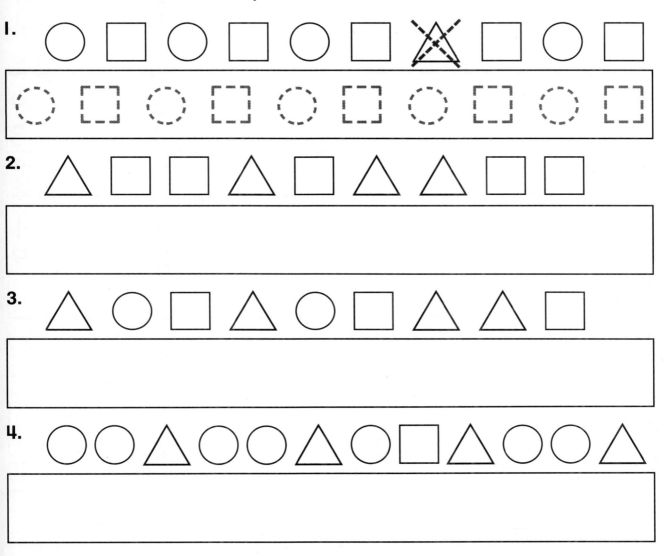

1.

2.

3.

4.

▶ Problem Solving

5. Write the numbers to continue the pattern.

   0   1   2   0   1   2   0   1   2   ___ ___ ___

6. Use 6, 7, and 8 to make your own number pattern.

___ ___ ___ ___ ___ ___ ___ ___ ___

Counting On to 12

Circle the greater number. Count on to add.

1.

$\begin{array}{r} 1 \\ + 8 \\ \hline 9 \end{array}$

$\begin{array}{r} 9 \\ + 2 \\ \hline \end{array}$

$\begin{array}{r} 6 \\ + 3 \\ \hline \end{array}$

$\begin{array}{r} 3 \\ + 2 \\ \hline \end{array}$

$\begin{array}{r} 7 \\ + 1 \\ \hline \end{array}$

2.

$\begin{array}{r} 9 \\ + 1 \\ \hline \end{array}$

$\begin{array}{r} 2 \\ + 4 \\ \hline \end{array}$

$\begin{array}{r} 8 \\ + 2 \\ \hline \end{array}$

$\begin{array}{r} 5 \\ + 3 \\ \hline \end{array}$

$\begin{array}{r} 9 \\ + 3 \\ \hline \end{array}$

3.

$\begin{array}{r} 8 \\ + 3 \\ \hline \end{array}$

$\begin{array}{r} 3 \\ + 9 \\ \hline \end{array}$

$\begin{array}{r} 2 \\ + 5 \\ \hline \end{array}$

$\begin{array}{r} 3 \\ + 2 \\ \hline \end{array}$

$\begin{array}{r} 1 \\ + 9 \\ \hline \end{array}$

4.

$2 + 7 = \underline{\hspace{1cm}}$

$7 + 3 = \underline{\hspace{1cm}}$

$8 + 2 = \underline{\hspace{1cm}}$

5.

$5 + 2 = \underline{\hspace{1cm}}$

$3 + 6 = \underline{\hspace{1cm}}$

$2 + 3 = \underline{\hspace{1cm}}$

6.

$3 + 9 = \underline{\hspace{1cm}}$

$4 + 3 = \underline{\hspace{1cm}}$

$1 + 7 = \underline{\hspace{1cm}}$

▶ **Problem Solving**

7. Martha had 5 dolls. She got 2 more. How many does she have in all? _____ dolls

Doubles to 12

Write the sums. Circle the doubles.

1.

$(4 + 4) = \underline{8}$ $6 + 4 = \underline{}$ $5 + 5 = \underline{}$

2.

$6 + 2 = \underline{}$ $6 + 6 = \underline{}$ $7 + 1 = \underline{}$

3.

$7 + 2 = \underline{}$ $3 + 3 = \underline{}$ $5 + 2 = \underline{}$

4.

$\begin{array}{r} 5 \\ + 3 \\ \hline \end{array}$ $\begin{array}{r} 5 \\ + 5 \\ \hline \end{array}$ $\begin{array}{r} 4 \\ + 2 \\ \hline \end{array}$ $\begin{array}{r} 2 \\ + 2 \\ \hline \end{array}$ $\begin{array}{r} 9 \\ + 2 \\ \hline \end{array}$

5.

$\begin{array}{r} 3 \\ + 3 \\ \hline \end{array}$ $\begin{array}{r} 8 \\ + 2 \\ \hline \end{array}$ $\begin{array}{r} 6 \\ + 6 \\ \hline \end{array}$ $\begin{array}{r} 3 \\ + 6 \\ \hline \end{array}$ $\begin{array}{r} 4 \\ + 4 \\ \hline \end{array}$

▶ **Problem Solving**

6. Caleb spent 6¢.
John spent 6¢.
How much did
they spend in all? _____ ¢

Three Addends

Use cubes. Write the sum.

1.
$$\begin{array}{r} 4 \\ 5 \\ + 0 \\ \hline 9 \end{array} \qquad \begin{array}{r} 4 \\ 3 \\ + 1 \\ \hline \end{array} \qquad \begin{array}{r} 6 \\ 6 \\ + 0 \\ \hline \end{array} \qquad \begin{array}{r} 4 \\ 5 \\ + 2 \\ \hline \end{array} \qquad \begin{array}{r} 6 \\ 1 \\ + 4 \\ \hline \end{array}$$

2.
$$\begin{array}{r} 5 \\ 3 \\ + 2 \\ \hline \end{array} \qquad \begin{array}{r} 3 \\ 2 \\ + 3 \\ \hline \end{array} \qquad \begin{array}{r} 3 \\ 4 \\ + 3 \\ \hline \end{array} \qquad \begin{array}{r} 2 \\ 5 \\ + 5 \\ \hline \end{array} \qquad \begin{array}{r} 2 \\ 3 \\ + 4 \\ \hline \end{array}$$

3.
$$\begin{array}{r} 2 \\ 1 \\ + 6 \\ \hline \end{array} \qquad \begin{array}{r} 3 \\ 3 \\ + 4 \\ \hline \end{array} \qquad \begin{array}{r} 3 \\ 5 \\ + 2 \\ \hline \end{array} \qquad \begin{array}{r} 1 \\ 1 \\ + 6 \\ \hline \end{array} \qquad \begin{array}{r} 2 \\ 5 \\ + 1 \\ \hline \end{array}$$

4.
$$\begin{array}{r} 7 \\ 3 \\ + 2 \\ \hline \end{array} \qquad \begin{array}{r} 4 \\ 2 \\ + 2 \\ \hline \end{array} \qquad \begin{array}{r} 1 \\ 3 \\ + 2 \\ \hline \end{array} \qquad \begin{array}{r} 7 \\ 4 \\ + 1 \\ \hline \end{array} \qquad \begin{array}{r} 5 \\ 2 \\ + 1 \\ \hline \end{array}$$

▶ **Problem Solving**

Circle the addition sentence that you think
has the greater sum. Solve to check.

5. $2 + 4 + 1 =$ _____

$5 + 1 + 2 =$ _____

6. $4 + 4 + 3 =$ _____

$5 + 0 + 5 =$ _____

Practice the Facts

Add. Color green the trees that have a sum of 10, 11, or 12.

1.

$$\begin{array}{r} 4 \\ 7 \\ +1 \\ \hline 12 \end{array}$$

$$\begin{array}{r} 7 \\ +2 \\ \hline \end{array}$$

$$\begin{array}{r} 2 \\ 5 \\ +2 \\ \hline \end{array}$$

$$\begin{array}{r} 3 \\ +5 \\ \hline \end{array}$$

$$\begin{array}{r} 6 \\ +6 \\ \hline \end{array}$$

2.

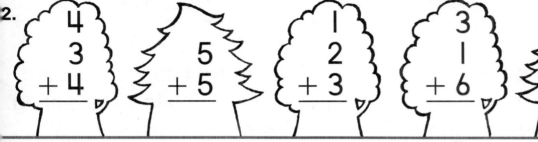

$$\begin{array}{r} 4 \\ 3 \\ +4 \\ \hline \end{array}$$

$$\begin{array}{r} 5 \\ +5 \\ \hline \end{array}$$

$$\begin{array}{r} 1 \\ 2 \\ +3 \\ \hline \end{array}$$

$$\begin{array}{r} 3 \\ 1 \\ +6 \\ \hline \end{array}$$

$$\begin{array}{r} 4 \\ +5 \\ \hline \end{array}$$

3.

$$\begin{array}{r} 2 \\ +5 \\ \hline \end{array}$$

$$\begin{array}{r} 8 \\ +4 \\ \hline \end{array}$$

$$\begin{array}{r} 5 \\ +6 \\ \hline \end{array}$$

$$\begin{array}{r} 2 \\ 7 \\ +3 \\ \hline \end{array}$$

$$\begin{array}{r} 6 \\ +3 \\ \hline \end{array}$$

4.

$$\begin{array}{r} 7 \\ +3 \\ \hline \end{array}$$

$$\begin{array}{r} 8 \\ +1 \\ \hline \end{array}$$

$$\begin{array}{r} 6 \\ +5 \\ \hline \end{array}$$

$$\begin{array}{r} 3 \\ 4 \\ +3 \\ \hline \end{array}$$

$$\begin{array}{r} 7 \\ 2 \\ +2 \\ \hline \end{array}$$

▶ **Problem Solving**

Circle the addition sentences that are correct.

5. $6 + 6 = 12$ $5 + 4 = 10$

$3 + 8 = 12$ $7 + 2 = 9$

Problem Solving • Act It Out

Act it out. Write the number sentence.

1.

5 ducks swam in the pond.
4 more ducks came to swim.
How many were swimming?

___5___ + ___4___ = ___9___

___9___ ducks

2.

6 cats played on the rug.
6 cats played on the bed.
How many were playing?

_____ + _____ = _____

_____ cats

3.

3 goats ran on the hill.
4 goats ran in the field.
How many were running?

_____ + _____ = _____

_____ goats

4.

7 white rabbits were eating.
3 brown rabbits were eating.
How many were eating?

_____ + _____ = _____

_____ rabbits

5.

3 frogs slept on a log.
8 frogs slept on a rock.
How many were sleeping?

_____ + _____ = _____

_____ frogs

6.

4 squirrels sat on a fence.
4 more squirrels came to sit.
How many were sitting?

_____ + _____ = _____

_____ squirrels

7. Which number sentence goes with the story? Circle it.

3 turtles were walking.
4 turtles were sleeping.
2 turtles were swimming.
How many turtles were there in all?

$3 + 4 + 2 = 9$

$3 + 4 + 1 = 8$

$5 + 2 + 2 = 9$

Relating Addition and Subtraction

Add. Then subtract.

1.

$8 + 4 = \underline{12}$

$12 - 4 = \underline{8}$

2.

$7 + 6 = \underline{\quad}$

$13 - 6 = \underline{\quad}$

3.

6	10	7	9	9	10
$+4$	-4	$+2$	-2	$+1$	-1

4.

5	8	9	11	8	10
$+3$	-3	$+2$	-2	$+2$	-2

▶ **Problem Solving**

5. Two numbers are added. The sum is 8. One number is 5. What is the other number? _____

6. Two numbers are added. The sum is 6. One number is 4. What is the other number? _____

Counting Back

▶ **Vocabulary**

Count back to subtract.
Use the number line if you need it.

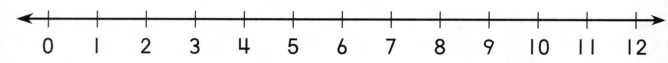

0   1   2   3   4   5   6   7   8   9   10   11   12

1.

11	9	12	7	6
− 3	− 1	− 2	− 2	− 1
8				

2.

10	7	9	8	12
− 2	− 1	− 3	− 1	− 3

3.

8	11	5	4	10
− 2	− 2	− 1	− 3	− 3

▶ **Problem Solving**

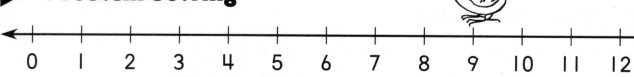

0   1   2   3   4   5   6   7   8   9   10   11   12

4. A number line was painted on the playground.
A bird was standing on number 9.
It took 3 hops back. What number was it on? _____

Compare to Subtract

Compare. Then subtract.

1.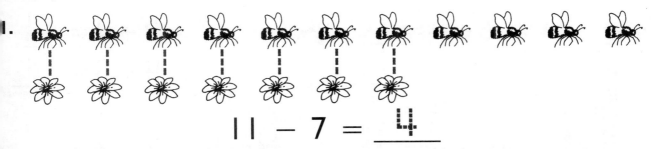

$$11 - 7 = \underline{4}$$

2.

$$10 - 8 = \underline{\hphantom{00}}$$

3.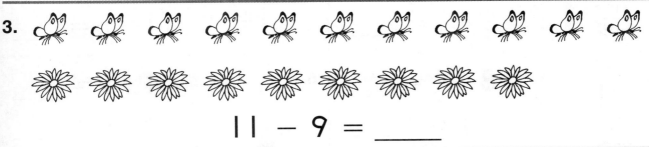

$$11 - 9 = \underline{\hphantom{00}}$$

4.

$$12 - 8 = \underline{\hphantom{00}}$$

▶ **Problem Solving**

5. Ashley has 12 flowers. Cody has 9 flowers. How many fewer flowers does Cody have?

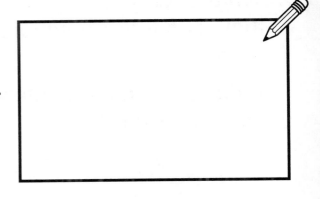

_____ fewer flowers

Fact Families

Add and subtract.

1.
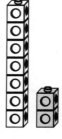
$$6 + 4 = \underline{10}$$
$$4 + 6 = \underline{10}$$
$$10 - 4 = \underline{6}$$
$$10 - 6 = \underline{4}$$

2.

$$3 + 4 = \underline{}$$
$$4 + 3 = \underline{}$$
$$7 - 4 = \underline{}$$
$$7 - 3 = \underline{}$$

3.
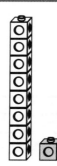
$$7 + 2 = \underline{}$$
$$2 + 7 = \underline{}$$
$$9 - 2 = \underline{}$$
$$9 - 7 = \underline{}$$

4.
$$5 + 6 = \underline{}$$
$$6 + 5 = \underline{}$$
$$11 - 6 = \underline{}$$
$$11 - 5 = \underline{}$$

5.
$$8 + 1 = \underline{}$$
$$1 + 8 = \underline{}$$
$$9 - 1 = \underline{}$$
$$9 - 8 = \underline{}$$

6.
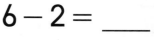
$$4 + 2 = \underline{}$$
$$2 + 4 = \underline{}$$
$$6 - 2 = \underline{}$$
$$6 - 4 = \underline{}$$

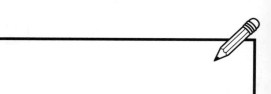

▶ **Problem Solving**

7. Write or draw a story problem that uses these numbers.

    7   3   10

Write the number sentence your story shows.

$$\underline{} \bigcirc \underline{} = \underline{}$$

Problem Solving • Write a Number Sentence

Write the number sentence the story problem shows.

1. There are 10 dogs.
   There are 7 cats.
   How many more dogs
   than cats are there?

 __3__ more dogs

 $\underline{10} \bigcirc\!\!-\!\!- \underline{7} = \underline{3}$

2. There are 9 goldfish.
   There are 7 guppies.
   How many more goldfish
   than guppies are there?

 ____ more goldfish

$\underline{} \bigcirc \underline{} = \underline{}$

3. Jenny had 6 cookies.
   She ate 3 of them.
   How many cookies
   does she have left?

 ____ cookies

$\underline{} \bigcirc \underline{} = \underline{}$

4. Jason had 2 apples.
   His grandmother gave
   him 3 more apples.
   How many apples does
   he have in all?

 ____ apples

$\underline{} \bigcirc \underline{} = \underline{}$

Tens

Write how many tens. Write the number.

1.

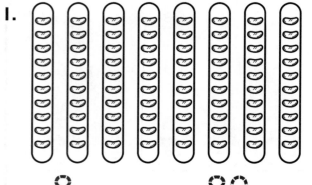

__8__ tens = __80__
             eighty

2.

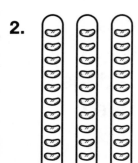

_____ tens = _____
              thirty

3.

_____ tens = _____
             twenty

4.

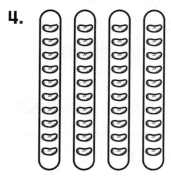

_____ tens = _____
              forty

▶ **Problem Solving**

5. Circle the box that has 60.

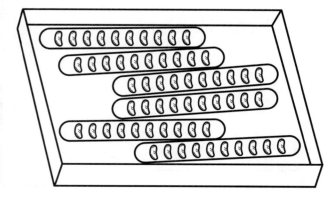
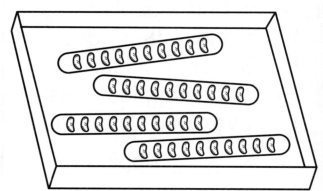

Tens and Ones to 20

▶ **Vocabulary**

1. Circle the **tens.**

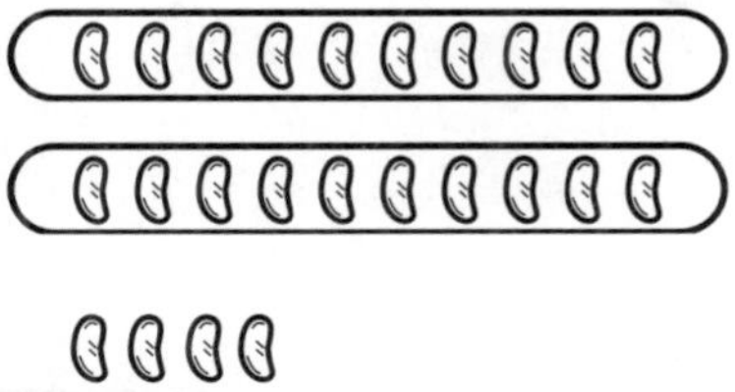

2. Circle the **ones.**

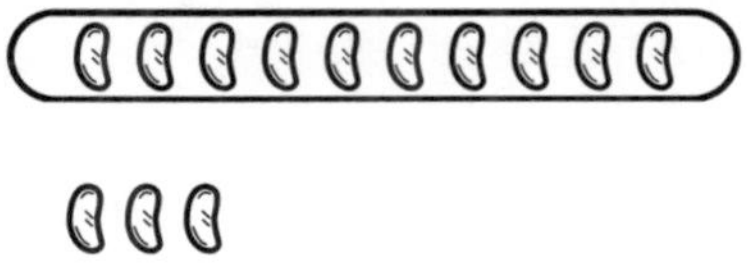

Write how many tens and ones. Write the number.

3.

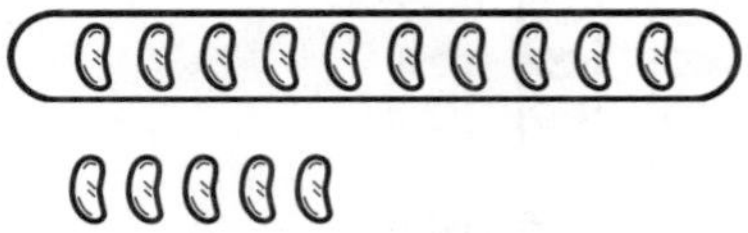

____1____ ten ____5____ ones = ____15____

4.

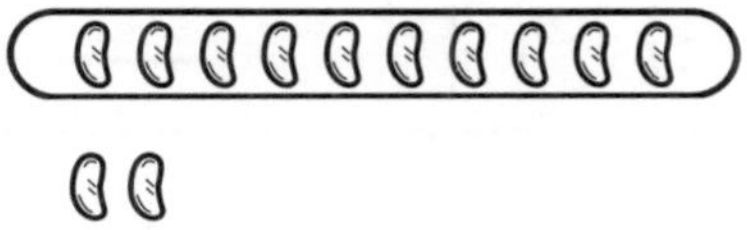

_____ ten _____ ones = _____

5.

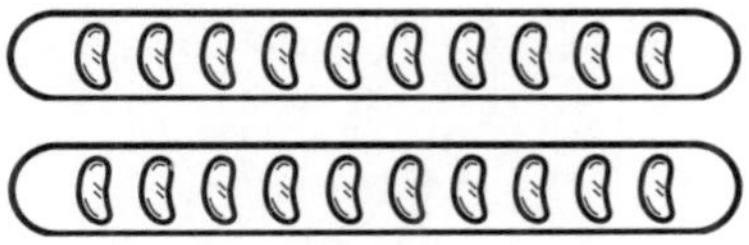

_____ tens _____ ones = _____

6.

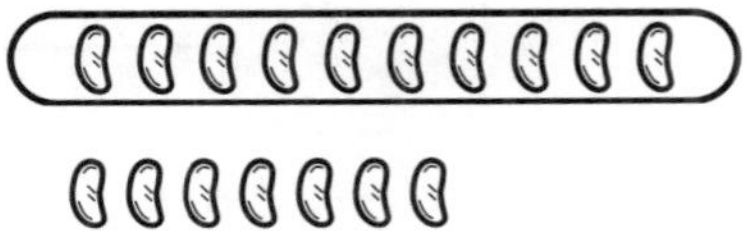

_____ ten _____ ones = _____

▶ **Problem Solving**

7. Joe has 10 toy cars.
   Mark gives him 2 more.
   How many toy cars does
   Joe have in all?

   _____ cars

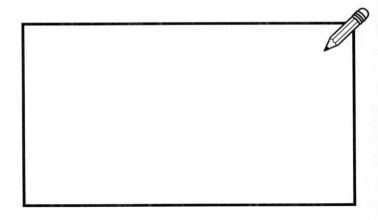

Tens and Ones to 50

Write how many.

1.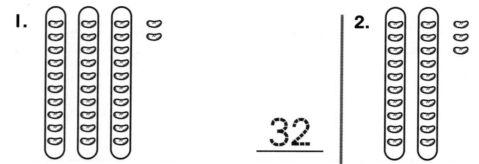

32

2.

_____

3.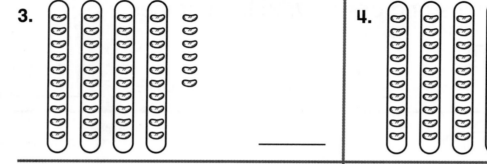

_____

4.

_____

5.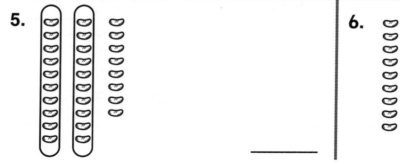

_____

6.

_____

▶ **Problem Solving**

Circle the box that has more.

7.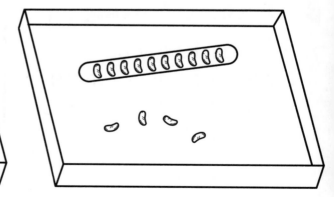

Tens and Ones to 80

Write the number.

1. 48

2. _____

3. _____

4. _____

5. _____

6. _____

▶ **Problem Solving**

Write the number.

7. Mary has 1 ten and 3 ones.
Joe has 3 tens and 1 one.
Write the number that tells
how many each one has.

Mary _____   Joe _____

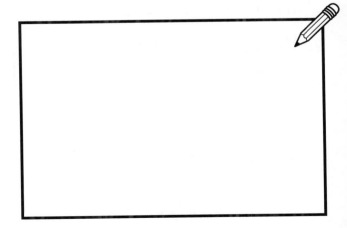

Tens and Ones to 100

Write the number.

1. 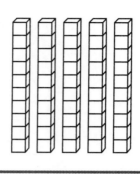 $\underline{51}$

2.   _____

3. 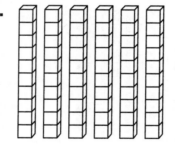 _____

4. 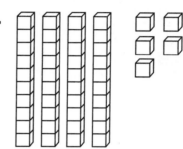 _____

5. 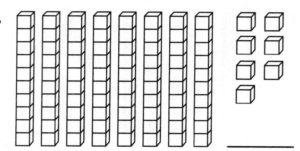 _____

6. 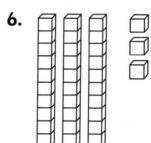 _____

▶ **Problem Solving**

Draw a picture to solve.

7. Kenda picked apples. She had 3 groups of 10 apples and 3 left over. How many apples did she have in all?

_____ apples

Estimating 10

Circle the better estimate.

1.

(more than 10)
fewer than 10

2.

more than 10
fewer than 10

3.

more than 10

fewer than 10

4.

more than 10

fewer than 10

▶ **Problem Solving**

5. Matt has more than 15 but fewer than 20 oranges. Write the numbers that tell how many oranges Matt could have.

____ ____ ____ ____

Ordinals

Match.

1. first   third   fifth   seventh   ninth   eleventh

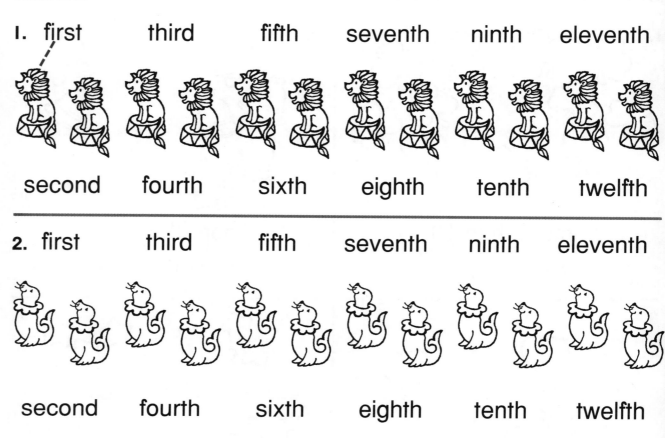

    second   fourth   sixth   eighth   tenth   twelfth

2. first   third   fifth   seventh   ninth   eleventh

    second   fourth   sixth   eighth   tenth   twelfth

▶ Problem Solving

Circle the answer.

3. Which animal is first?

    rabbit   dog   duck   turtle

4. Which animal is third?

    rabbit   dog   duck   turtle

LESSON
14.2

Greater Than

▶ **Vocabulary**

Write the numbers. Circle the **greater** number.

I.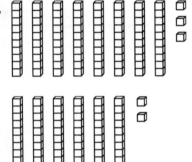

50

25

2. _____

_____

3. _____

_____

4. _____

_____

▶ **Problem Solving**

5. Bill has 2 dogs. Marc has more dogs than Bill.
   Circle the boy that is Marc.

6. The bus has 21 people on it. The plane
   has 40 people on it. Circle the one
   with the greater number on it.

Less Than

▶ Vocabulary

Write the numbers. Circle the number that is **less.**

1.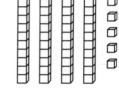

 45

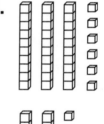 (43)

2. _____

_____

3. _____

_____

4. _____

_____

▶ Problem Solving

5. Circle the one who has the most pennies.

Jess   Sue   Pat   Bill

6. Mark an **X** on the one who has fewer pennies than Jess.

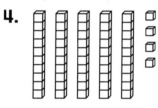

	Jess	Sue	Pat	Bill
5				🪙
4				🪙
3		🪙		🪙
2	🪙	🪙		🪙
1	🪙	🪙	🪙	🪙
0	Jess	Sue	Pat	Bill

Before, After, Between

▶ Vocabulary

33 is just **before 34.**

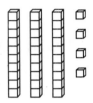

34 is **between 33** and **35.**

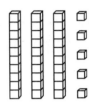

36 is just **after 35.**

Complete the tables.

before		after
1. 44	45	46
2. ____	60	____
3. ____	87	____
4. ____	23	____
5. ____	59	____
6. ____	11	____
7. ____	36	____
8. ____	98	____
9. ____	70	____

between		
10. 46	____	48
11. 83	____	85
12. 19	____	21
13. 60	____	62
14. 55	____	57
15. 97	____	99
16. 78	____	80
17. 25	____	27
18. 89	____	91

▶ Problem Solving

Write the numbers in order.

19. | 25 | 26 | 24 |
|---|---|---|

____ ____ ____

20. | 55 | 53 | 54 |
|---|---|---|

____ ____ ____

Order to 100

▶ **Vocabulary**

Write the numbers.
Then write them in order from **least** to **greatest.**

1.

8
__8__

28
__15__

15
__28__

38
__38__

Write the numbers in order from least to greatest.

2. 57   59   53   55
    53
    ___   ___   ___   ___

3. 32   52   62   42

    ___   ___   ___   ___

4. 22   40   39   54

    ___   ___   ___   ___

5. 61   58   41   73

    ___   ___   ___   ___

▶ **Problem Solving**

6. Write three numbers that are
    between 52 and 57
    and that come after 53.   ___ ___ ___

Counting by Tens

Count by tens. Write how many.

1.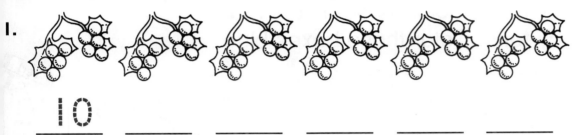

_10_ _____ _____ _____ _____ _____

2.

_____ _____ _____ _____ _____ _____

▶ Problem Solving

Count by tens to fill in the table.
Use the table to answer the questions.

Megan has 20 pennies on Sunday.
She saves 10 pennies every day for one week.

Sunday	Monday	Tuesday	Wednesday	Thursday	Friday	Saturday
20						

3. How many pennies does she have on Tuesday?

_____ pennies

4. How many pennies does she have on Friday?

_____ pennies

5. How many pennies does she have on Saturday?

_____ pennies

Counting by Fives

1. Write the missing numbers.
   Count by fives. Color those boxes red.
   Count by tens. Color those boxes blue.

1	2	3	4	5	6	7	8	9	10
11	12	13	14		16	17	18	19	
21	22	23	24		26	27	28	29	
31	32	33	34		36	37	38	39	
41	42	43	44		46	47	48	49	
51	52	53	54		56	57	58	59	
61	62	63	64		66	67	68	69	
71	72	73	74		76	77	78	79	
81	82	83	84		86	87	88	89	
91	92	93	94		96	97	98	99	

▶ **Problem Solving**

2. Circle the numbers that are greater than 50.

    80   30   90   40   20

Counting by Twos

Count by twos. Write the missing numbers.

1.

1	2	3	4	5		7		9	
11		13		15		17		19	
21		23		25		27		29	
31		33		35		37		39	
41		43		45		47		49	
51		53		55		57		59	
61		63		65		67		69	
71		73		75		77		79	
81		83		85		87		89	
91		93		95		97		99	

2. My number is between 40 and 50. It is 2 more than 45. What is my number? ____

3. My number is between 80 and 90. It is 2 more than 87. What is my number? ____

Even and Odd Numbers

▶ **Vocabulary**

Circle **even** or **odd**.

1.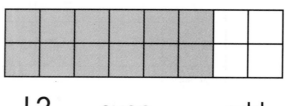

12   even   odd

2.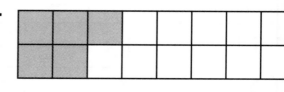

5   even   odd

Color the squares to show each number. Circle **even** or **odd**.

3.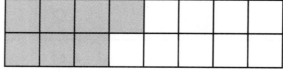

7   even   (odd)

4.

4   even   odd

5.

14   even   odd

6.

9   even   odd

▶ **Problem Solving**

Circle **even** or **odd**.

7. Ann has 2 🚲.
Each 🚲 has 2 ⦾.
Does she have an even or
odd number of ⦾?

even   odd

Pennies and Nickels

▶ Vocabulary

1. Circle the **penny**.
2. Cross out the **nickel**.

Count. Write the amount.

3.

___**1**___ ¢, ___**2**___ ¢, ___**3**___ ¢   **3** ¢

4.

_____ ¢, _____ ¢, _____ ¢, _____ ¢, _____ ¢, _____ ¢   ⬜ ¢

5.

_____ ¢, _____ ¢   ⬜ ¢

6.

_____ ¢, _____ ¢, _____ ¢   ⬜ ¢

▶ Problem Solving

Circle the greater amount.

7.

Pennies and Dimes

▶ Vocabulary

1. Circle the **penny.**
2. Cross out the **dime.**

Count by tens. Write the amount.

3.

   <u>10</u> ¢, <u>20</u> ¢

   [20] ¢

4.

   ___ ¢, ___ ¢, ___ ¢, ___ ¢

   [ ] ¢

5.

   ___ ¢, ___ ¢, ___ ¢, ___ ¢, ___ ¢

   [ ] ¢

6.

   ___ ¢, ___ ¢, ___ ¢

   [ ] ¢

7.

   ___ ¢, ___ ¢, ___ ¢, ___ ¢, ___ ¢, ___ ¢, ___ ¢

   [ ] ¢

▶ Problem Solving

Circle the least amount.

8.

ounting Collections of Nickels and Pennies

Count by fives. Then count on by ones.
Write the amount.

      8 ¢

2.   ☐ ¢

3.   ☐ ¢

 4.   ☐ ¢

▶ **Problem Solving**

Mark an **X** on the greater amount.

5.

6.

Counting Collections of Dimes and Pennies

Count by tens. Then count on by ones.
Write the amount.

1.   **31** ¢

2.   ☐ ¢

3.      ☐ ¢

4.   ☐ ¢

5.   ☐ ¢

▶ **Problem Solving**

6. Lucy wants to buy a paint set.
It costs 43¢. Circle the coins Lucy needs.

 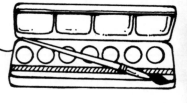

Problem Solving • Choose the Model

Which two groups in each row add up
to the amount on the tag? Color them.

▶ Problem Solving

5. You have

Circle the toy you can buy.

Trading Pennies, Nickels, and Dimes

Trade for nickels and dimes. Use the fewest coins.
Draw how many you have.

1.

2.

3.

4.

▶ Problem Solving

5. Wayne bought a watch.
He used 4 nickels.

Did he use the fewest
coins that equal 20¢? _____

Show the price using
the fewest coins.

Equal Amounts

Show the amount in 2 ways.
Circle the way that uses the fewest coins.

1. 25¢ | (10¢) (10¢) (5¢) | (10¢) (5¢) (5¢) (5¢)

2. 15¢

3. FARM ANIMALS 35¢

▶ Problem Solving

4. Lance needs 30¢ to buy a notebook.
Mark an **X** on the groups that do not equal 30¢.

Which way uses the fewest coins to show 30¢? Circle it.

How Much Is Needed?

Circle the coins you need. Use the fewest coins.

1.

2.

3.

4.

▶ **Problem Solving**

5. Ruben has 15 🪙.
He wants to trade his
pennies for other coins.
Show the fewest coins
he can have.

Quarter

► Vocabulary

Circle the **quarter**.

Write each amount. Circle the coins that equal a .

1.

_25_ ¢

2.

_____ ¢

3.

_____ ¢

4.

_____ ¢

5.

_____ ¢

6.

_____ ¢

► Problem Solving

7. Nathan wants to buy a .
It costs 25¢.
Circle the coins he needs.

Problem Solving • Act It Out

Play store. Work with a partner.
Use the fewest coins to buy things.
Take turns.

Draw what you bought.	Draw the coins you used.
1.	
2.	

Ordering Months and Days

FEBRUARY

Sunday	Monday	Tuesday	Wednesday	Thursday	Friday	Saturday
1	2	3	4	5	6	7
8	9	10	11	12	13	14
15	16	17	18	19	20	21
22	23	24	25	26	27	28

Write the days of the week in order.

1. _____

2. _____

3. _____

4. _____

5. _____

6. _____

7. _____

8. Color the Tuesdays **blue**.

▶ Problem Solving

9. The ball game is on the day before Saturday. Write the day.

_____

10. Lee's birthday is in the last month of the year. Circle the month.

October   December

Reading the Calendar

Fill in the calendar for next month.
Use the calendar to answer the questions.

_____

Sunday	Monday	Tuesday	Wednesday	Thursday	Friday	Saturday

1. On what day does
   the month end?   _____

2. What is the date of
   the first Sunday?   _____

3. What is the date of
   the first Friday?   _____

▶ Problem Solving

4. Mike's birthday is on May 7.
   This year May 6 is on Thursday.
   On what day of the week is   _____
   Mike's birthday?

Ordering Events

Draw something special you do on each of these days.

Saturday night
Sunday morning
Monday afternoon

▶ Problem Solving

1. Circle the month that comes before December.

   January   November   February

2. Write the month that comes
   after October.   _____

Estimating Time

Circle the one that takes longer to do.

1.

2.

3.

▶ **Problem Solving**

4. Tyler and Sarah live next to each other.
   Tyler rides his bike home from school.
   Sarah walks home.
   Does it take more time for
   Tyler or Sarah to get home?

   _____
   _____
   _____

Reading the Clock

Use your clock. Show the time.
Write the time two ways.

1.

__l__ o'clock

__l:00__

2.

____ o'clock

___:___

3.

____ o'clock

___:___

4.

____ o'clock

___:___

5.

____ o'clock

___:___

6.

____ o'clock

___:___

▶ **Problem Solving**

7. It is 7 o'clock. Jenny has to go to bed in one hour.

What time does Jenny go to bed? Write the time two ways.

____ o'clock

___:___

Hour

Write the time.

1.

| 12:00 |

2.

| : |

3.

| : |

4.

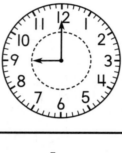

| : |

5.

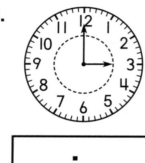

| : |

6.

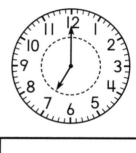

| : |

7.

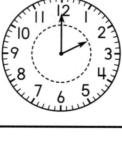

| : |

8.

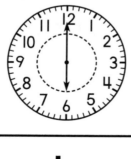

| : |

9.

| : |

▶ **Problem Solving**

10. Write the time on the clock so that it shows 1 hour later than 6 o'clock.

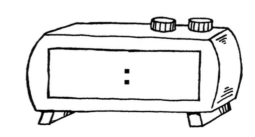

Hour

▶ **Vocabulary**

Draw the **hour hand** and the **minute hand**.

1.
6:00

2.
10:00
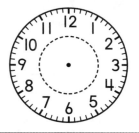

3.
3:00
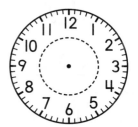

4.
12:00
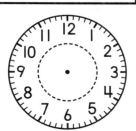

5.
7:00
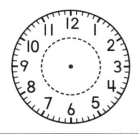

6.
1:00
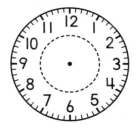

7.
8:00
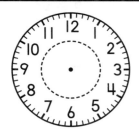

8.
2:00
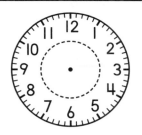

9.
4:00
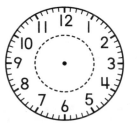

▶ **Problem Solving**

10. Jonathan eats dinner at 6 o'clock.
He goes to bed 2 hours later.
Write the time he goes to bed.

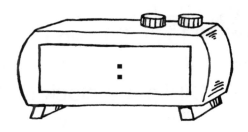

Name _____

Half Hour

Write the time.

1.

5:30

2.

_____:_____

3.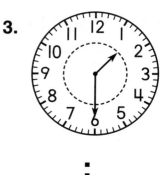

_____:_____

4.

_____:_____

5.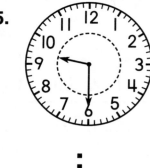

_____:_____

6.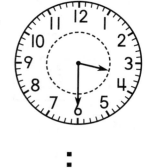

_____:_____

7.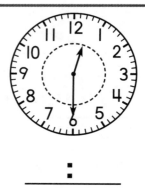

_____:_____

8.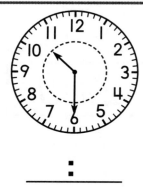

_____:_____

9.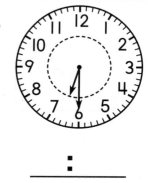

_____:_____

▶ **Problem Solving**

10. The movie starts at 7:30.
It lasts for two hours.
What time is the movie over?
Circle the clock that shows
when the movie is over.

Problem Solving • Act It Out

About how long would it take? Circle your estimate.
Then act it out to see if you are right.

1. put 10 chairs in a circle

(more than a minute)
less than a minute

2. put a stamp on a letter

more than a minute
less than a minute

3. open a door

more than a minute
less than a minute

4. write 10 spelling words

boat
cat

more than a minute
less than a minute

5. read a big book

more than a minute
less than a minute

6. sharpen a pencil

more than a minute
less than a minute

Using Nonstandard Units

Estimate. Then use 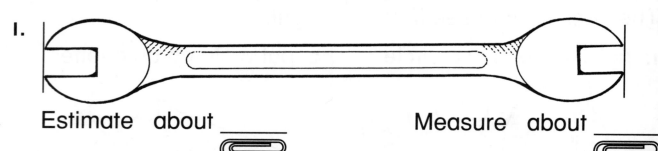 to measure.

1.

Estimate about _____   Measure about _____

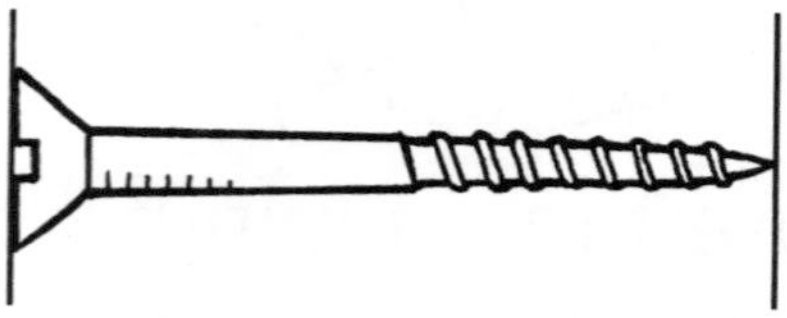

2.

Estimate about _____   Measure about _____

3.

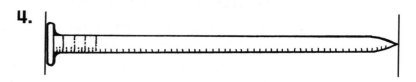

Estimate about _____   Measure about _____

4.

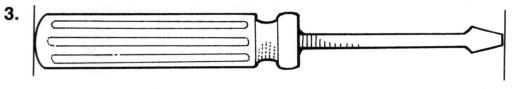

Estimate about _____   Measure about _____

▶ **Problem Solving**

5. Use and to measure.
Circle which way uses more.

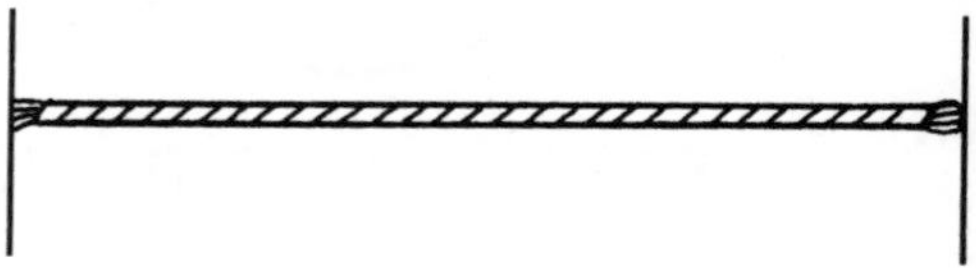

Measuring in Inch Units

▶ Vocabulary

1. Circle the pencil that is 1 **inch** long.

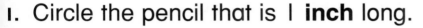

Count the inch units. Write how many inches long.

2.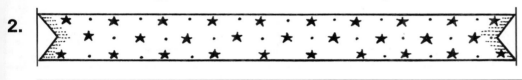

_____ _____ _____ _____ _____ _____

<u>5</u> inches

3.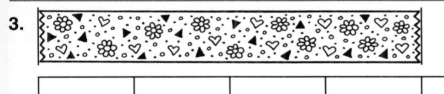

_____ _____ _____ _____ _____ _____

_____ inches

4.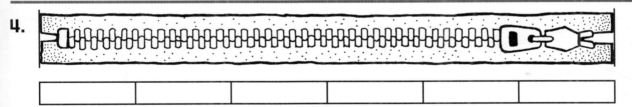

_____ _____ _____ _____ _____ _____

_____ inches

▶ Problem Solving

5. One 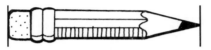 is about 1 inch long. About how many inches long are 3 ? Draw a line to show.

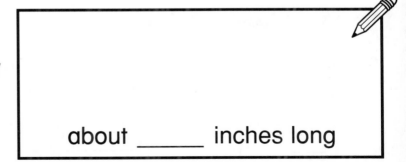

about _____ inches long

Using an Inch Ruler

You will need: objects, an inch ruler
Estimate. Then use an inch ruler to measure.

Object	Estimate	Measure
1.	about ____ inches	about ____ inches
2.	about ____ inches	about ____ inches
3.	about ____ inches	about ____ inches
4.	about ____ inches	about ____ inches

▶ Problem Solving

5. Measure each chain. If you joined the two chains, how long would the new chain be?

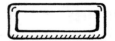      _____ inches

Measuring in Centimeter Units

▶ Vocabulary

Measure. Circle the rope that is 1 **centimeter** long.

___

How many centimeters long?
Count the centimeter units. Write how many.

1.

_____ _3_ centimeters

2.

_____ centimeters

3.
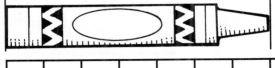

_____ centimeters

4.

_____ centimeters

▶ Problem Solving

5. Draw a 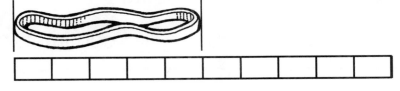 10 centimeters long.

Using a Centimeter Ruler

You will need: objects, a centimeter ruler
Estimate. Then use a centimeter ruler to measure.

Object	Estimate	Measure
1.	about _____ centimeters	about _____ centimeters
2.	about _____ centimeters	about _____ centimeters
3.	about _____ centimeters	about _____ centimeters
4.	about _____ centimeters	about _____ centimeters

▶ Problem Solving

5. Use a centimeter ruler. Measure the sides of the rectangle.

Side A

Side B

Side A _____ centimeters

Side B _____ centimeters

Using a Balance

▶ **Vocabulary**

1. Circle the object that is **heavier.**

2. Circle the object that is **lighter.**

You will need: a . Work with a partner. Find each object. Is the object heavier or lighter than a bottle of glue?

Estimate. Write **H** for heavier. Write **L** for lighter. Then use a  to measure. Write H or L.

Object	Estimate	Measure
3.		
4.		
5.		

▶ **Problem Solving**

6. Ashley has 2 cups. One is full of marbles. One is full of chalk. Circle the cup that is heavier.

Using Nonstandard Units

You will need: a ⟍⟋ and ⬚

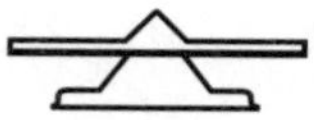

Find each object. About how many  ⬚ does it take
to balance the scale? Estimate. Then measure.

Object	Estimate	Measure
1. 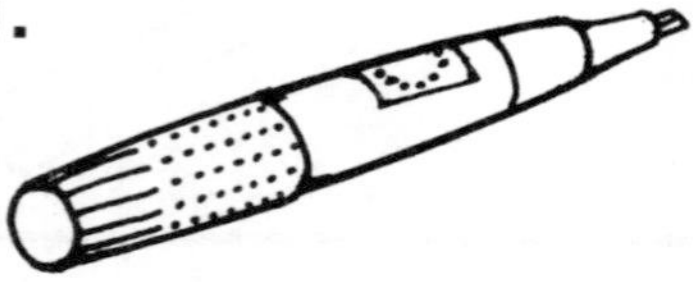	about _____ ⬚	about _____ ⬚
2. 	about _____ ⬚	about _____ ⬚
3. 	about _____ ⬚	about _____ ⬚
4. 	about _____ ⬚	about _____ ⬚

▶ **Problem Solving**

Look at your measures for the objects.

5. Draw a picture of
   the heaviest object.

6. Draw a picture of
   the lightest object.

Measuring with Cups

About how many cups of rice does
each object hold? Estimate. Then measure.

Object	Estimate	Measure
1.	about _____ cups	about _____ cups
2.	about _____ cups	about _____ cups
3.	about _____ cups	about _____ cups
4. Quart	about _____ cups	about _____ cups

▶ **Problem Solving**

Look at the container.
Draw a container beside it that holds more.

5.

6.

Temperature
Hot and Cold

Circle the picture that shows something hot.

I.

2.

Circle the picture that shows something cold.

3.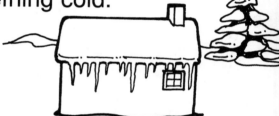

4.

▶ **Problem Solving**

5. Draw something hot.

6. Draw something cold.

Equal and Unequal Parts of Wholes

Vocabulary

1. Circle the figure that shows **equal parts.**

2. Mark an **X** on the one that does not show equal parts.

Circle the figures that show equal parts.

3.

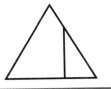 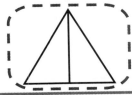 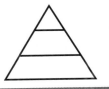

4.

5.

 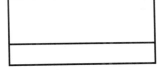

6.

  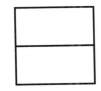

▶ Problem Solving

Draw lines to show where you would cut this cake.

7. Each child wants an equal share.

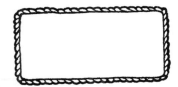

Halves

Find the figures that show halves. Color $\frac{1}{2}$ red.

1.
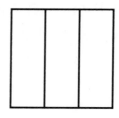 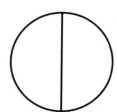 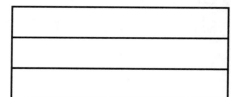

2.
 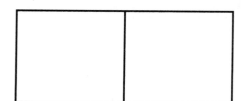 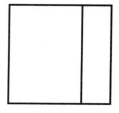

3.
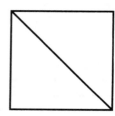 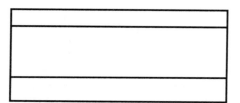 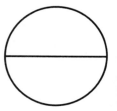

4.
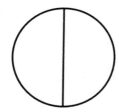 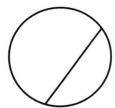 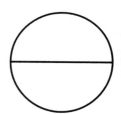

▶ **Problem Solving**

5. Two rabbits shared 4 carrots. Each ate one half of the 4 carrots. How many carrots did each rabbit eat?

_____ carrots

Fourths

Color one part . Circle the fraction.

1.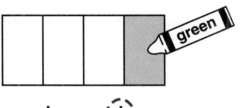

$\frac{1}{2}$ $\left(\frac{1}{4}\right)$ $\frac{1}{2}$ $\frac{1}{4}$ $\frac{1}{2}$ $\frac{1}{4}$

2.

$\frac{1}{2}$ $\frac{1}{4}$ $\frac{1}{2}$ $\frac{1}{4}$ $\frac{1}{2}$ $\frac{1}{4}$

3.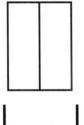

$\frac{1}{2}$ $\frac{1}{4}$ $\frac{1}{2}$ $\frac{1}{4}$ $\frac{1}{2}$ $\frac{1}{4}$

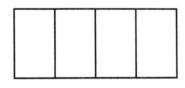

▶ Problem Solving

Draw lines. Then color one part
to show the fraction.

4.  $\frac{1}{2}$

5. $\frac{1}{4}$

Thirds

Color one part 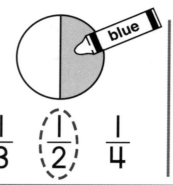. Circle the fraction.

1.

$\frac{1}{3}$ $\left(\frac{1}{2}\right)$ $\frac{1}{4}$ $\frac{1}{3}$ $\frac{1}{2}$ $\frac{1}{4}$ $\frac{1}{3}$ $\frac{1}{2}$ $\frac{1}{4}$

2.

$\frac{1}{3}$ $\frac{1}{2}$ $\frac{1}{4}$ $\frac{1}{3}$ $\frac{1}{2}$ $\frac{1}{4}$ $\frac{1}{3}$ $\frac{1}{2}$ $\frac{1}{4}$

3.

$\frac{1}{3}$ $\frac{1}{2}$ $\frac{1}{4}$ $\frac{1}{3}$ $\frac{1}{2}$ $\frac{1}{4}$ $\frac{1}{3}$ $\frac{1}{2}$ $\frac{1}{4}$

▶ Problem Solving

What part is left? Circle the fraction.

4.  $\frac{1}{3}$ $\frac{1}{2}$ $\frac{1}{4}$

5. 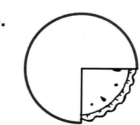 $\frac{1}{3}$ $\frac{1}{2}$ $\frac{1}{4}$

Visualizing Results

Think about sharing this pie.
Circle the picture that answers the question.

1. There are 3 children. Each gets an equal share. How would you cut the pie?

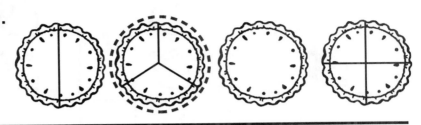

2. There are 2 children. Each gets an equal share. How would you cut the pie?

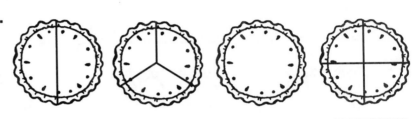

3. There are 4 children. Each gets an equal share. How much is an equal share?

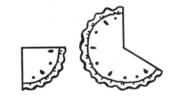

▶ Problem Solving

Draw lines to show the answer.

4. Robin and Rico got a small pizza. They want equal shares. How should they cut the pizza?

5. Bryan, Miranda, and their dad made a pie. They want equal shares. How should they cut the pie?

Parts of Groups

Color to show each fraction.

1.

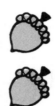

$\frac{1}{2}$

2.

$\frac{1}{4}$

3.

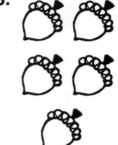

$\frac{1}{2}$

4.

$\frac{1}{3}$

▶ **Problem Solving**

Circle the animals to show the fraction.

5. There are 6 puppies.

How many puppies

are $\frac{1}{3}$ of the group?

6. There are 4 kittens.

How many kittens

are $\frac{1}{2}$ of the group?

P118 ON MY OWN

Sort and Classify

This table shows one way
these toys can be sorted.

Cars and Trucks	
cars	ⲧⲏⲧ Ⲓ
trucks	ⲧⲏⲧ

Each Ⲓ stands for 1 toy.
ⲧⲏⲧ stands for 5 toys.

Sort the toys another way.
Make a table.

Problem Solving

Where is this fish shown
on the table? Circle the row.

Kinds of Fish	
🐟	‖
🐟	‖
🐟	‖

Certain or Impossible

Look at the pocket.

Circle the pictures
that show what
can come out of it.

1.

2.

3.

4.

Most Likely

You will need: I bag, 6 red cubes,
5 blue cubes, and I yellow cube

Color the cubes
red, blue, and yellow.

Put the cubes into the bag.
Take out one cube.

Make a tally mark on the table
to show which color you got.

Put the cube back into the bag.
Shake. Make a prediction.
If you do this 9 more times,
which color do you think you will
get most often? Circle that color.

red   **blue**   **yellow**

Do this 9 more times.

Make a tally mark each time.
Count the tally marks for
each color.

Write the totals.

	Tally Marks	Total
red		
blue		
yellow		

▶ Problem Solving

Can you take a △ out of the ?

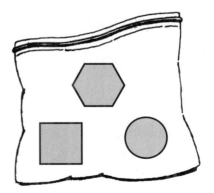

Circle **Yes** or **No.**

     Yes   No

Tallying Events

You will need: I bag, 5 red cubes, 3 blue cubes

Color the cubes. Predict which color cube you will get more often. Circle that cube.

Try it. Put all the cubes into the bag. Color the cubes in the table. Take out a cube. Make a tally mark.

 red   blue

Put the cube back into the bag.

Shake the bag. Do this 10 times.

	Tally Marks	Total
red		
blue		

Try again with these cubes.

You will need: I bag, 2 red cubes, 7 blue cubes

Color the cubes. Predict which color cube you will get more often. Circle that cube.

Try it. Color the cubes in the table. Put all the cubes into the bag. Take out a cube. Make a tally mark.

 red   blue

Put the cube back into the bag.

Shake the bag. Do this 10 times.

	Tally Marks	Total
red		
blue		

Picture Graphs

bear	🧸	🧸	🧸	🧸	🧸
car	🚗	🚗			
doll	🪆	🪆	🪆	🪆	

Count the toys. Draw ◯ to fill in the graph.

Our Favorite Toys				
bear	◯	◯	◯	◯	◯
car					
doll					

Use the graph to answer the questions.

1. How many cars are there? _____

2. How many more bears than cars are there? _____

_____

3. Are there more dolls or cars? _ _ _ _ _ _ _ _ _ _

_____

Problem Solving

Look at the graph.

4. Write a number sentence that tells how many bears and dolls there are.

_____ ◯ _____ = _____

_____ bears and dolls

Name _____

Horizontal Bar Graphs

A group of children voted for their
favorite sports. Write how many tally marks.

Favorite Sport		Total
soccer	ⵌ︲︲	7
softball	ⵌ	
football	ⵏ︲	

Color the graph to match the tally marks.

Favorite Sport							
soccer							
softball							
football							

  0   1   2   3   4   5   6   7

Use the graph to answer the questions.

1. How many children voted for soccer? _____

2. How many more voted for soccer than for football? _____

3. How many more voted for soccer than for softball? _____

▶ **Problem Solving**

Look at the graph.

4. Write a number sentence that
   tells how many more children
   like soccer than like football.

_____ ◯ _____ = _____

_____ more children

Vertical Bar Graphs

Write how many tally marks.
Color the graph to match the
tally marks.

Where We Went for Vacation		Total
beach	ꟷꟷꟷꟷ IIII	9
city	ꟷꟷꟷ	
farm	IIII	

Where We Went for Vacation

	beach	city	farm
10			
9			
8			
7			
6			
5			
4			
3			
2			
1			
0	beach	city	farm

Use the graph to answer
the questions.

1. How many children went to the beach?   _____9_____

2. How many children went to the farm?   _____

3. How many more children went to the beach
   than to the farm?   _____

▶ **Problem Solving**

4. Circle the question you can answer by reading the graph.

How many children
went to the mountains?

How many children
went to the city?

Problem Solving • Make a Graph

Ask 10 classmates to choose their favorite color.

1. Make a tally mark for each choice. Then write how many.

2. Fill in the graph. First write the title. Then color the graph to match the tally marks.

Our Favorite Color		Total
red		
blue		
green		
yellow		

Graph (y-axis: 8, 7, 6, 5, 4, 3, 2, 1, 0; x-axis: red, blue, green, yellow)

Use the graph to answer the questions.

3. Which color do the most children like best? — — — — — — — — —

4. How many children like yellow the best? _____

5. Write a question someone can answer by reading this graph.

_____

_____

_____

Doubles Plus One

1. Circle the **doubles** fact.

$4 + 4 = 8$ $4 + 3 = 7$ $4 + 5 = 9$

2. Circle the **doubles plus one** fact.

$4 + 4 = 8$ $4 + 3 = 7$ $4 + 5 = 9$

Write the sums.

3. $3 + 3 = 6$,   so $3 + 4 =$ _7_.

4. $8 + 8 = 16$,   so $8 + 9 =$ ___.

5. $6 + 6 = 12$,   so $6 + 7 =$ ___.

6. $2 + 2 = 4$,   so $2 + 3 =$ ___.

7. $4 + 4 = 8$,   so $4 + 5 =$ ___.

Write the sums.

8.
$$\begin{array}{cccccc} 7 & 8 & 5 & 5 & 4 & 1 \\ +7 & +9 & +5 & +6 & +4 & +1 \\ \hline \end{array}$$

▶ Problem Solving

Use counters to solve. Draw them.

9. Bill has 5 marbles. He finds 6 more marbles. How many marbles does he have in all?

___ marbles

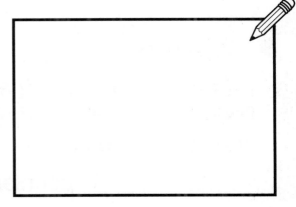

Doubles Minus One

1. Circle the **doubles** fact.

$3 + 4 = 7$ $3 + 3 = 6$ $3 + 2 = 5$

2. Circle the **doubles minus one** fact.

$3 + 4 = 7$ $3 + 3 = 6$ $3 + 2 = 5$

Write the sums.

3. $4 + 4 = \underline{8}$ | $6 + 6 = \underline{}$ | $3 + 3 = \underline{}$

    $4 + 3 = \underline{7}$ | $6 + 5 = \underline{}$ | $3 + 2 = \underline{}$

4. $5 + 5 = \underline{}$ | $9 + 9 = \underline{}$ | $7 + 7 = \underline{}$

    $5 + 4 = \underline{}$ | $9 + 8 = \underline{}$ | $7 + 6 = \underline{}$

5.
$$\begin{array}{cccccc} 9 & 2 & 7 & 8 & 6 & 5 \\ +8 & +3 & +8 & +9 & +7 & +6 \\ \hline \end{array}$$

6.
$$\begin{array}{cccccc} 7 & 5 & 4 & 4 & 8 & 3 \\ +6 & +4 & +3 & +5 & +7 & +2 \\ \hline \end{array}$$

▶ **Problem Solving**

7. Sue has 4 pennies. She finds 5 more. How many does she have in all?

____ pennies

Doubles Patterns

Write the sums.

doubles	doubles − 1	doubles + 1
1. $4 + 4 = \underline{8}$	$4 + 3 = \underline{}$	$4 + 5 = \underline{}$
2. $7 + 7 = \underline{}$	$7 + 6 = \underline{}$	$7 + 8 = \underline{}$
3. $9 + 9 = \underline{}$	$9 + 8 = \underline{}$	$9 + 10 = \underline{}$
4. $6 + 6 = \underline{}$	$6 + 5 = \underline{}$	$6 + 7 = \underline{}$
5. $3 + 3 = \underline{}$	$3 + 2 = \underline{}$	$3 + 4 = \underline{}$
6. $5 + 5 = \underline{}$	$5 + 4 = \underline{}$	$5 + 6 = \underline{}$
7. $8 + 8 = \underline{}$	$8 + 7 = \underline{}$	$8 + 9 = \underline{}$

▶ **Problem Solving**

Look at the coins. Write the number sentence.

8.  + =

_____¢ + _____¢ = _____¢

9. +  =

_____¢ + _____¢ = _____¢

Doubles Fact Families

Add or subtract.

1.

$\begin{array}{r} 5 \\ +5 \\ \hline 10 \end{array}$
$\begin{array}{r} 10 \\ -5 \\ \hline 5 \end{array}$
$\begin{array}{r} 4 \\ +4 \\ \hline \end{array}$
$\begin{array}{r} 8 \\ -4 \\ \hline \end{array}$
$\begin{array}{r} 7 \\ +7 \\ \hline \end{array}$
$\begin{array}{r} 14 \\ -7 \\ \hline \end{array}$

2.

$\begin{array}{r} 6 \\ +6 \\ \hline \end{array}$
$\begin{array}{r} 12 \\ -6 \\ \hline \end{array}$
$\begin{array}{r} 1 \\ +1 \\ \hline \end{array}$
$\begin{array}{r} 2 \\ -1 \\ \hline \end{array}$
$\begin{array}{r} 3 \\ +3 \\ \hline \end{array}$
$\begin{array}{r} 6 \\ -3 \\ \hline \end{array}$

3.

$\begin{array}{r} 2 \\ +2 \\ \hline \end{array}$
$\begin{array}{r} 4 \\ -2 \\ \hline \end{array}$
$\begin{array}{r} 9 \\ +9 \\ \hline \end{array}$
$\begin{array}{r} 18 \\ -9 \\ \hline \end{array}$
$\begin{array}{r} 8 \\ +8 \\ \hline \end{array}$
$\begin{array}{r} 16 \\ -8 \\ \hline \end{array}$

4.

$\begin{array}{r} 8 \\ -4 \\ \hline \end{array}$
$\begin{array}{r} 4 \\ +4 \\ \hline \end{array}$
$\begin{array}{r} 4 \\ -2 \\ \hline \end{array}$
$\begin{array}{r} 2 \\ +2 \\ \hline \end{array}$
$\begin{array}{r} 10 \\ -5 \\ \hline \end{array}$
$\begin{array}{r} 5 \\ +5 \\ \hline \end{array}$

▶ **Problem Solving**

5. I had 18 pennies.
I lost 9 of them.
How many pennies
do I have left?

____ pennies

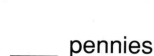

Problem Solving • Make a Model

Use counters to solve. Draw them.

1. Robert has 7 pencils.
   Sara has 1 fewer than Robert.
   How many pencils
   do they have in all?

   __13__ pencils

2. Lisa has 4 dolls. Kara has
   two times as many.
   How many dolls do
   they have in all?

   _____ dolls

3. John had 14 boats. He gave
   some of them away. He has
   7 left. How many did
   he give away?

   _____ boats

▶ **Problem Solving**

4. I have 8 toy cars.
   My friend has the same
   number. How many cars
   do we have in all?

   _____ cars

Make a 10

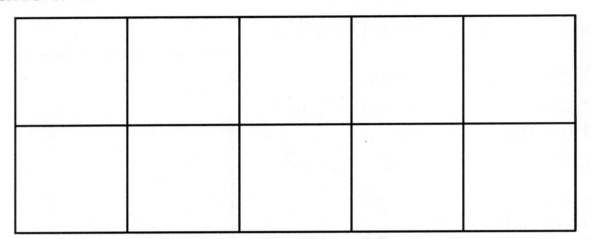

Use counters and the 10-frame. Start with the
greater number. Make a 10. Then add.

1.
$$\begin{array}{r} 3 \\ +9 \\ \hline 12 \end{array}$$
$$\begin{array}{r} 8 \\ +5 \\ \hline \end{array}$$
$$\begin{array}{r} 5 \\ +9 \\ \hline \end{array}$$
$$\begin{array}{r} 3 \\ +8 \\ \hline \end{array}$$
$$\begin{array}{r} 9 \\ +7 \\ \hline \end{array}$$
$$\begin{array}{r} 6 \\ +8 \\ \hline \end{array}$$

2.
$$\begin{array}{r} 8 \\ +7 \\ \hline \end{array}$$
$$\begin{array}{r} 9 \\ +3 \\ \hline \end{array}$$
$$\begin{array}{r} 7 \\ +9 \\ \hline \end{array}$$
$$\begin{array}{r} 4 \\ +8 \\ \hline \end{array}$$
$$\begin{array}{r} 3 \\ +9 \\ \hline \end{array}$$
$$\begin{array}{r} 6 \\ +7 \\ \hline \end{array}$$

3.
$$\begin{array}{r} 8 \\ +6 \\ \hline \end{array}$$
$$\begin{array}{r} 7 \\ +4 \\ \hline \end{array}$$
$$\begin{array}{r} 3 \\ +8 \\ \hline \end{array}$$
$$\begin{array}{r} 3 \\ +9 \\ \hline \end{array}$$
$$\begin{array}{r} 9 \\ +6 \\ \hline \end{array}$$
$$\begin{array}{r} 7 \\ +5 \\ \hline \end{array}$$

▶ **Problem Solving**

4. Mack had 9 pencils.
His dad gave him 2 more.
How many pencils does
he have in all?

_____ pencils

Adding Three Numbers

Circle names for 10 or doubles. Then add.

1.

```
   1          3          6          7          2
  (8)         3          5          7          8
 +(8)       + 6        + 4        + 2        + 5
 ----       ----       ----       ----       ----
  17
```

2.

```
   3          1          8          7          5
   7          7          2          4          5
 + 2        + 7        + 1        + 3        + 1
 ----       ----       ----       ----       ----
```

3.

```
   9          2          9          6          4
   2          8          3          6          3
 + 1        + 6        + 1        + 3        + 4
 ----       ----       ----       ----       ----
```

▶ **Problem Solving**

4. Jan has 8 yellow leaves,
2 red leaves, and 6 brown
leaves. How many leaves
does she have in all?

_____ leaves

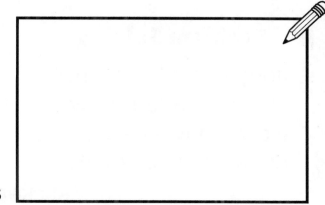

Sums and Differences to 14

Use Workmat 2 and counters. Add or subtract.

1.

9	10	8	11	5	10
$+\ 1$	$-\ 1$	$+\ 3$	$-\ 3$	$+\ 5$	$-\ 5$
10	9				

2.

8	13	7	14	6	12
$+\ 5$	$-\ 5$	$+\ 7$	$-\ 7$	$+\ 6$	$-\ 6$

3.

9	14	4	10	9	12
$+\ 5$	$-\ 5$	$+\ 6$	$-\ 6$	$+\ 3$	$-\ 3$

4.

9	11	8	14	5	9
$+\ 2$	$-\ 2$	$+\ 6$	$-\ 6$	$+\ 4$	$-\ 4$

▶ **Problem Solving**

5. Joey has 14 stickers.
He gives 6 to Randy.
How many stickers
does Joey have left?

_____ stickers

Sums and Differences to 18

Write the sum and difference for each pair.

1.

9	18	8	14	6	12
+9	−9	+6	−6	+6	−6
18	9				

2.

8	11	9	13	7	13
+3	−3	+4	−4	+6	−6

3.

9	16	6	11	6	14
+7	−7	+5	−5	+8	−8

4.

6	15	9	12	6	13
+9	−9	+3	−3	+7	−7

▶ **Problem Solving**

5. I found 17 shells. I gave
away 9. How many
shells do I have left?

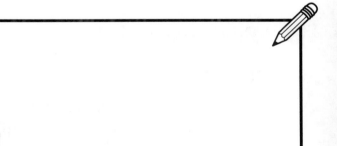

_____ shells

Counting Equal Groups

Use counters. Draw them. Write how many in all.

1. Make 2 groups. Put 3 counters in each group.

How many in all? ___6___

2. Make 3 groups. Put 2 counters in each group.

How many in all? _____

3. Make 2 groups. Put 4 counters in each group.

How many in all? _____

4. Make 4 groups. Put 3 counters in each group.

How many in all? _____

▶ **Problem Solving**

5. Jessica has 3 dogs. She gave them 2 bones each. How many bones did Jessica need?

_____ bones

How Many in Each Group?

Use counters. Draw them. Write how many in each group.

. Use 10 counters. Make 5 equal groups.

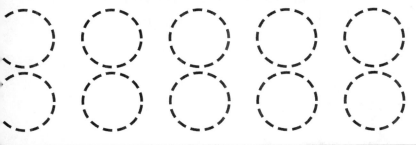

How many in
each group? __2__

. Use 12 counters. Make 2 equal groups.

How many in
each group? ____

Problem Solving

3. Dylan gave 4 pictures to his brother and sister. He gave each the same number. How many pictures did he give to each?

sister _____ brother _____

4. Jenny's grandmother gave 12 cookies to 3 children. She gave each child the same number of cookies. How many cookies did each child get?

_____ cookies

How Many Groups?

Use counters. Draw them. Write how many groups.

1. Use 12 counters.
   Put 3 in each group.

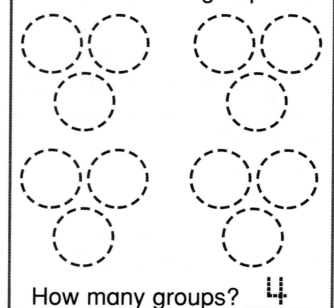

How many groups? __4__

2. Use 8 counters.
   Put 2 in each group.

How many groups? _____

▶ **Problem Solving**

3. The teacher had 6 apples.
   She put 2 apples on each
   plate. How many plates did
   she use?

   _____ plates

4. Jason had 10 sugar cubes.
   He gave 5 to each horse.
   How many horses did
   he feed?

   _____ horses

roblem Solving • Draw a Picture

Draw a picture to solve each problem.

1. There are 2 children.
   Each child has 3 balloons.
   How many balloons are there?

   _____6_____ balloons

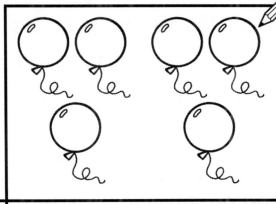

2. We have 3 pennies.
   We get 2 more.
   How many pennies
   in all?

   _____ pennies

3. There are 4 baskets.
   Each basket has 3 eggs in it.
   How many eggs are there?

   _____ eggs

4. There are 6 crayons.
   Each child gets 2 crayons.
   How many children
   get crayons?

   _____ children

Adding and Subtracting Tens

 Vocabulary

Circle the Workmat that shows 4 **tens.**

tens	ones
	▱ ▱
	▱ ▱

tens	ones
▤▤▤▤	

Add or subtract. Use tens and Workmat 3.

1.

$$\begin{array}{r} 40 \\ + 20 \\ \hline 60 \end{array}$$
$$\begin{array}{r} 70 \\ + 10 \\ \hline \end{array}$$
$$\begin{array}{r} 50 \\ + 20 \\ \hline \end{array}$$
$$\begin{array}{r} 30 \\ + 20 \\ \hline \end{array}$$
$$\begin{array}{r} 30 \\ + 10 \\ \hline \end{array}$$

2.

$$\begin{array}{r} 40 \\ - 30 \\ \hline \end{array}$$
$$\begin{array}{r} 90 \\ - 30 \\ \hline \end{array}$$
$$\begin{array}{r} 70 \\ - 30 \\ \hline \end{array}$$
$$\begin{array}{r} 80 \\ - 20 \\ \hline \end{array}$$
$$\begin{array}{r} 60 \\ - 40 \\ \hline \end{array}$$

▶ **Problem Solving**

3. Ann had 40¢ to buy a pencil. The pencil cost 30¢. How much money does Ann have left?

_____ ¢

Adding Tens and Ones

Add.

1.

tens	ones
3	2
+ 4	1
7	**3**

tens	ones
5	7
+ 3	1

tens	ones
4	2
+ 2	1

tens	ones
6	4
+ 3	5

2.

tens	ones
1	6
+ 2	3

tens	ones
7	4
+ 1	2

tens	ones
2	3
+ 3	5

tens	ones
1	2
+ 6	5

3.

tens	ones
3	1
+ 3	4

tens	ones
3	5
+ 4	3

tens	ones
8	5
+ 1	3

tens	ones
1	7
+ 3	2

▶ Problem Solving

4. Elaine wants to buy a book
and a pencil. How much
money does she need?

75¢

12¢

_____ ¢

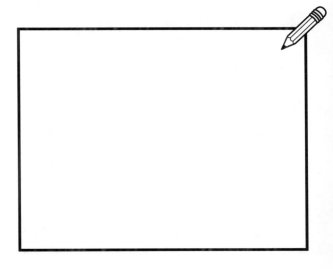

Subtracting Tens and Ones

Subtract.

1.

tens	ones
4	2
− 3	2
1	0

tens	ones
5	2
− 3	1

tens	ones
7	6
− 5	4

tens	ones
6	2
− 2	0

2.

tens	ones
5	4
− 2	1

tens	ones
9	6
− 1	1

tens	ones
7	3
− 4	3

tens	ones
2	2
− 1	1

3.

tens	ones
5	7
− 2	5

tens	ones
8	6
− 1	3

tens	ones
7	2
− 3	2

tens	ones
4	2
− 3	2

▶ **Problem Solving**

Circle the answer.

4. Jessica had 75 buttons.
She gave 12 buttons to
Tyler. How many buttons
does she have left?

54   36   63

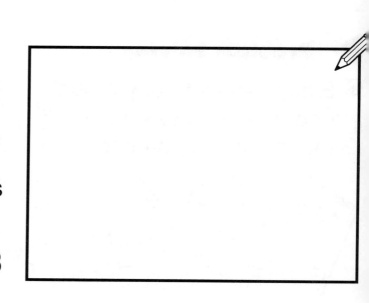

Reasonable Answer

Circle the answer that makes sense.

1. Chris had 17 books.
He gave 12 to the library.
How many books does
Chris have now?

55 books

5 books

555 books

2. There were 35 children at
the zoo. 12 children went
home. How many children
are left?

650 children

76 children

23 children

3. Steve had 13 stickers.
Then he bought 20 more.
How many stickers does
he have now?

5 stickers

133 stickers

33 stickers

4. Rose saw 6 squirrels on the
fence. Then she saw 12
more in the grass. How many
squirrels were there in all?

18 squirrels

6 squirrels

118 squirrels

▶ Problem Solving

Circle the answer.

5. Juan has 35¢.
He wants to buy a toy
car that costs 22¢.
How much money will
he have left?

35¢   22¢   13¢

6. Sandy had 45 pennies.
Her mother gave her
23 more. How many
pennies does Sandy
have now?

21¢   45¢   68¢